# Company P&L Economics

*Economic Measures for Managing Revenue, Costs, and Profitability*

By

William F. Christopher

ISBN-10: 1478184671
EAN-13: 9781478184676.

# TABLE OF CONTENTS

# PREFACE

Business people know about accounting concepts, methods, and measures. Accounting numbers provide an information resource for business decisions. However, there is another, different discipline that provides a much more informative resource for business decisions. This different discipline is economics, Company P&L Economics--the economics of company operations. Company P&L Economics can be used in any company and in any business unit. In a large corporation, this economics discipline provides information needed for the management of each P&L business unit that is part of the corporation.

Company P&L Economics provides concepts, methods, and measures different from the accounting concepts, methods, and measures. These different measures provide much more useful information for management. They not only provide reliable current measures. They also provide information on how these measures are changing, and why.

More than half a century ago, Joel Dean, a professor at Columbia University, pioneered the application of economics concepts, methods, and measures in the management of a business enterprise. He summarized his work in his seminal book, *Managerial Economics*, (Prentice-Hall, 1951).

I studied with Joel at Columbia University. Then, in my first job with General Electric, I quickly learned:

1.  Managers in General Electric, and in other companies, too, knew a lot about accounting.
2.  Managers knew nothing about business economics. None of them knew anything about what Joel Dean wrote about in his book, *Managerial Economics*.

I began using this new economics in my work. Over my career I have used this new economics in more than fifty companies, in sixteen countries. I now use the term, Company P&L Economics, as a title for this new economics of company operations. From many years of experience, the discipline described in this book was developed and applied, always with success.

There is no conflict between accounting and economics. They are used for different purposes. Accounting is used for financial reporting. Economics is used as an information resource for management decisions.

Companies use accounting for their financial reporting. However, for management decisions, managers in companies using this new economics, Company P&L Economics, will have an additional, and much more useful information resource.

# Chapter 1

# A New Management Technology —
# Company P&L Economics

This book opens new windows on cost and profit management. The book describes a new management technology that gives decision makers the concepts, methods, and measures they need to manage revenue, costs, and profitability to achieve desired goals. This new management technology provides information that helps all decision-makers act in ways that will control costs in relation to cash earned, and manage income to achieve desired goals. The new technology: Company P&L Economics.

Company P&L Economics applies the discipline of economics in the operations of a business enterprise. A related discipline, managerial economics, has been developing in the academic community for more than half a century. Leading business schools offer courses, and degrees. Managerial economics covers a broad range, including profitability. However, it does not include the concepts, methods, and measures offered in Company P&L Economics for controlling costs in relation to cash earned, and managing income to achieve desired goals.

Company P&L Economics might be considered a further development of a part of managerial economics. This new economics has been used, always with success, in more than a hundred businesses in the "more than fifty companies" mentioned in the Preface. Company P&L Economics is a proven technology for controlling costs in relation to cash earned, and for managing income to achieve desired goals. However, Company P&L Economics is not yet widely known and used in the practice of management.

The economics described in this book gives us new, different, and better principles, methods, and measures for controlling costs and achieving desired operating income. But no one discipline provides all the answers. Company P&L Economics works because it combines with other disciplines, too, especially:

- Marketing and sales
- New product/service development
- Accounting and finance
- Manufacturing
- Engineering
- Human Resources leadership and management

Marketing and sales is especially important. Sales revenue is the top line on the income statement. Company P&L Economics helps company people improve the top line in two ways:

1. Using the principles, methods, and measures of Company P&L Economics, company people will discover ways to increase sales revenue.
2. Company P&L Economics will also help company people find ways to increase the profitability of sales revenue.

Company P&L Economics involves all business functions in controlling costs and managing income to achieve desired goals. All participate. All achieve.

All management people and all decision-makers can use the concepts and the measures of Company P&L Economics to act in ways that will control costs and achieve desired operating income. The concepts are easy to learn. The data needed are already in the company's chart of accounts and product cost data. The data are the same as the data collected for accounting and financial reporting. But Company P&L Economics uses these data in very different ways. All company people who make decisions involving costs, or make decisions that affect revenue can easily learn and apply Company P&L Economics in their day-to-day decisions. All company decision-makers can easily learn and use this new economics.

## WHERE TO USE COMPANY P&L ECONOMICS

Company P&L Economics is designed for P&L business units that produce and market products and/or services to customers. This definition includes:

- Companies, subsidiaries, and business units that are P&L operating units producing and marketing products and/or services to customers
- P&L businesses within the above companies, subsidiaries, and business units
- P&L companies that do not have decentralized P&L operating units
- Start-up companies
- Any P&L business producing and marketing products and/or services to customers

In a large corporation with decentralized P&L operating units, company P&L economics is not useful at the corporate level. It can, however, be used at the corporate level for managing corporate fixed costs. For managing operating income, Company P&L Economics is used in the operating units.

While not used at the corporate level, the corporate level does have an important responsibility for Company P&L Economics. The corporate level can instruct people in the operating units on the concepts, methods, and measures of Company P&L Economics. Corporate will continue to require the conventional accounting reports. These are needed for the company's financial reporting. Corporate can also require Company P&L Economics reporting as an information resource for management.

In the corporations I worked for, I was the corporate marketing executive. I had studied managerial economics at the Columbia University Graduate School of Business. Managerial economics includes some of the ideas, methods, and measures that I now call Company P&L Economics. But more information, and some simplification was needed. Application experience over the years has provided this information and this simplification. This book presents this new, easy to understand and apply Company P&L Economics. Company P&L Economics enables decision-makers at all levels to control cost in relation to cash available, and manage all the variables to best achieve the desired operating income.

## THE NEW CAPITALISM

Over the decades of the 1970s and 80s capitalism began changing. Earlier, capitalism provided the capital resources to start a company, expand a company, finance a company's operations, and advise and finance mergers, acquisitions, and divestitures. The companies served were organized for a purpose—to provide a desired value to their customers. In 1906 Ford built a car that everyone could buy, and put Americans on wheels. In 1998 Google organized the world's information and made it easily available to everyone. Companies compete in providing value to customers.

Then the new capitalism began to appear. A new discipline was invented—financial engineering. Financial engineering required advanced mathematics and high-speed computing, and an absence of ethics. Financial engineering does not think about customers. Financial engineering thinks only about profit, whatever the consequences.

Financial engineering is not something that happened on Wall Street. Financial engineering has a more honorable heritage—academia. The nation's top graduate business schools discovered financial engineering. Financial engineering required the schools' capabilities in advanced mathematics, finance, and high-speed computing. Bright students could earn a Ph.D. in financial engineering. Then, employed by a Wall Street firm, they could apply this new financial engineering to create profits for their firms, and wealth for themselves.

Over the last years of the 20th century and the early years of the 21st century, financial engineering invented collateralization, collateralized debt obligations, synthetic collateralized debt obligations, structured investment vehicles, credit default swaps, naked credit default swaps, and exotic over-the-counter derivatives, that made big profits for a few, and big losses for many.

Financial engineering also provides the tools used by huge new aggregations of capital—private equity funds, hedge funds, and investment funds of many kinds. However, the investment products created by financial engineering do not create wealth. Nor do the financial engineering tools used by the great aggregations of capital create wealth. Their goal is to redistribute wealth ... to themselves and to their investors.

Private equity funds revalue before redistributing. Here we see a difference between economics and financial engineering. The target company of a private equity fund might have a market capitalization of $8 billion. The private equity fund might offer shareholders a 25% premium for their stock, offering to buy the company for $10 billion. Economics sees no change in wealth; the target company hasn't changed. But financial engineering has seen an opportunity, by their methods, to create a significant profit on their small part of the $10 billion investment, plus big fees. Most of the $10 billion investment is financed by low-interest loans, which become company debt. The private equity firm gets an over-size return on its small part of the total investment.

In addition to its return on its investment, the private equity fund applies its management skills in removing funds from the company and distributing these funds to themselves and their investors. Financial engineering enables private equity to increase debt, one company at a time, and redistribute much of these funds to themselves and their investors.

In the end the company buys itself, and has a large debt on its balance sheet. While interest rates are very low, this debt may be manageable. What will happen in these highly-indebted companies when interest rates rise? Interest rates near zero are not typical of our economy. Over recent decades interest rates have varied from low to more than 10%.

The private equity fund managers, of course, want the target company to succeed. They can then financially engineer a very profitable

IPO. To help assure success the fund managers typically increase scale by merger, acquisitions, and/or increased investment. These actions also increase private equity fees.

The redistribution of wealth from the many to the few is happening in all countries.

For the future we will need more of the innovations that create new products and new services that create values for customers and wealth for the economy, and for investors. We will want fewer of the financial engineering kind of innovations that redistribute existing wealth to the few.

The new capitalism has changed companies, too. Company orientation to the market and to creating value for customers has changed. The new orientation is to the company's shareholders, and creating wealth for these investors. The purpose of the company changes from creating value for customers to creating wealth for shareholders.

Which of these two commitments to purpose works best for the company?

> **Purpose 1:** The purpose of our company is to create and profitably market unique product and service values for our customers.
> **Purpose 2:** The purpose of our company is to create wealth for our shareholders.

If we choose purpose 1, we know what we need to do and we can structure and operate the company to do it. If we choose purpose 2, we have no idea what to do until we come up with some idea along the lines of purpose 1. So purpose 1 is our choice. While purpose 1 is our purpose, we can have as one of several goals, a goal for increasing shareholder income.

Today's management might say that our company was founded forty years ago. We make and successfully market products that satisfy our customers. Now we have to think about our shareholders. Our purpose is purpose 2. OK. If that's our purpose, what do we do? The VP Finance might decide to take wealth out of the company and give it to shareholders. But that would increase debt, and reduce expenses needed to maintain present operations and create the company's future.

Cash now could mean less profit tomorrow. Purpose I provides the best results for customers, company people, and shareholders.

Company P&L Economics requires purpose I. Company P&L Economics is more than economics and finance. The creative actions and the corrective actions of Company P&L Economics use also the disciplines of marketing and sales and other functions. Company P&L Economics involves all company people and all company functions .The effort of all company people is needed to control costs continuously in relation to cash earned and to, consistently, best achieve desired profitability.

## SOME NEW COMPANY P&L ECONOMICS IDEAS

Management typically manages costs in a budget process dealing individually with all the costs listed in the company's chart of accounts. In this system all cost accounts are reviewed annually during the budget process. Managers propose their budgets for the coming year, typically proposing increases in some of the accounts. Whatever is approved by top management becomes the budget for the year.

Company P&L Economics offers two new ideas:

1.  Companies budget for the fiscal year. But companies manage hour-by-hour, day-by-day, week-by-week, month-by-month, con- tinuously. Company P&L Economics offers the methods and the measures for controlling costs and managing income hour-by- hour, day-by-day, week-by-week, month-by-month, continuously.
2.  Companies manage costs separately from everything else. Company P&L Economics concepts and measures manage costs in relation to everything else.

These are powerful ideas that make Company P&L Economics ef- fective in helping decision-makers manage all the variables that deter- mine operating income:

1.  Total sales revenue
2.  Total variable costs

**3.** The value added in the total sales revenue
**4.** Average value added percent
**5.** Total fixed costs

All five of these measures are essential for controlling costs and managing operating income. Managers today see only item 1, total sales revenue for each reporting period. This number provides very little information. There is no information on the component parts of total sales revenue, including markets, channels of distribution, customer groups, major customers, and area sales. Nor is there information on how to improve the profitability of sales revenue. Company P&L Economics provides this information.

Managers today do not see measures 2, 3, 4, and 5. These measures are unseen, unknown, unused, and unmanaged. Management P&L Economics provides these measures. Using these measures, as explained in this book, company people can effectively control costs and manage profitability to achieve desired company objectives. The interactions of all the above determine operating income.

All five of these measures matter. All interrelate. Using Company P&L Economics the company's decision-makers manage all at the same time. This book explains how.


## VALUE ADDED

Value added is the reason for the company to exist. Companies exist to create value. They create value in the products and services they sell to their customers. The measure of the value companies create is value added. The whole company structure, all the company people, all the company capital investment—land, buildings, machinery and equipment—are there to create value. The measure of value is value added.

The prices the customers pay provide sales revenue to the company. Sales revenue first pays all the variable costs incurred to produce the products or services sold. The balance, after variable costs are paid, is value added. This value added pays all fixed costs—people costs, capital costs, and programmed fixed costs. After paying fixed costs, the balance, if positive, is operating income; if negative, operating loss.

The company, if a manufacturing company, buys materials, parts, components, screws, rivets, power, and other items fabricated into the products they make, or consumed in making them. The costs of the items on this parts list for each product are the variable costs for producing the product. For a manufacturing company, these variable costs will likely be in the range of 45 to 55% of sales revenue. Value added will be 55 to 45%. For a service company, variable costs may be close to zero. For a service company, If variable costs are zero, value added will be 100% of sales revenue.

The difference between variable costs paid to other companies for the materials, parts, and energy used to produce the products sold, and sales revenue is the value added. For a manufacturing company, if variable costs average 48% of sales revenue, value added is 52% of sales revenue. For a service company, if variable costs are zero, value added is 100% of sales revenue. All the company's fixed costs, including all people costs and all capital costs, exist to create this value added.

A service company, such as a law firm or a consulting firm, may have few if any variable costs. Their value added will be at or near 100% of sales revenue. Both manufacturing companies and service companies will have fixed costs—people costs, capital costs, and programmed fixed costs.

## VALUE FOR CUSTOMERS? OR, VALUE FOR SHAREHOLDERS?

Was the company created to create value for customers, or value for shareholders? However this question is answered, very quickly it becomes obvious that the only way to create value for shareholders is to be successful in creating value for customers. In 1906 Henry Ford invented the assembly line, significantly reduced the cost of a motor car, and built cars that everyone could buy. Ford's Model T sold for one-third the cost of other cars. Ford created value for customers. Investors prospered. In 1998 Google announced a search engine that made access to information fast and easy. Google provided value for users. Investors prospered. Successfully creating value for customers brings business success, and investor success.

All companies exist to create value for customers. Every company is a structure of people and capital facilities designed to produce and sell specific products or services. Not operating, the company is a structure of fixed costs. But it is operating. It operates continuously, creating value for customers. And in creating value for customers the company earns the value added needed to pay the fixed costs and earn an operating income.

Figure 1 illustrates these relationships for a manufacturing company with variable costs, and for a service company with no variable costs. Each has an operating income of $12 million. The manufacturing company has sales revenue $96 million, with a value added of $44 million, 45.8% of sales revenue. This value added pays the fixed costs of $32 million and provides an operating income of $12 million.

**Figure 1**
**Value Added and Operating Income**
**Manufacturing company & Service Company**
**$ Millions**

| OI 12 | Sales 96 |
|-------|----------|
|       | VA 44 45.8% |
| FC 32 |          |

| OI 12 | Sales 62 |
|-------|----------|
|       | VA 62 100% |
| FC 50 |          |

| VC 52 |
|-------|

**Sales Revenue**     **Sales Revenue**

Manufacturing Company    Service Company
with Variable Costs    with No Variable Costs

FC- Fixed Costs
VC- Variable Costs
OI- Operating Income
VA- Value Added

The service company has sales revenue of $62 million which pays fixed costs of $50 million and provides operating income of $12 million.

These examples are typical. Successful companies create value for customers. The value created is value added. From this value added the company pays its fixed costs. All company costs are either variable costs or fixed costs. Variable costs are paid by sales revenue. Value added pays all fixed costs. After fixed costs are paid, the remainder of the value added, if positive, is operating income; if negative, operating loss.

Company economics keeps a watchful eye on all these key measures:

1. Total sales revenue, and components of total sales revenue
2. Total variable costs in total sales revenue and in the components of total sales revenue
3. Value added in total sales revenue and components of total sales revenue
4. Average value added percent in total sales revenue and in the components of total sales revenue
5. Total fixed costs
6. Operating income

All are manageable, using the principles and measures of Company P&L Economics, as explained in this book. None are managed in conventional cost management. Key relationships are expressed in the following two formulas:

Total Sales Revenue – Variable Costs in this Sales Revenue
= Value Added

Value Added – Total Fixed Costs = Operating Income

Using Company P&L Economics, we expand cost management to cost control and profit management, and involve all company functions in the process.

# TYPICAL COST MANAGEMENT

The typical assumption in conventional cost management and profit improvement seems to be:

Cost Reduction = Profit Improvement

Experience shows that cost reduction has a range of consequences which may or may not include profit improvement. When companies have a profit problem, all that management learns from the financial reports is: Profit problem! Decision-makers see no information on why the profit problem happened, or how to fix it. Decision-makers have only their own experience and judgment to deal with the problem. Typically they order cost reductions. And the biggest available cost reductions are people costs; layoffs. Such cost reductions have many consequences, which may include profitability and other performance areas, too. Chapter 8 includes an example of a cost reduction program undertaken to reduce a projected loss, with the cost reduction causing a greater loss, and the death of the company.

New products are created. Profit, like new products, is created. Costs can be managed in relation to everything else. Variable costs, sales mix, and pricing can be managed to achieve the desired average value added percent. Fixed costs can be managed to totals that can be paid with the company's value added dollars, with a satisfactory margin remaining. The margin remaining after fixed costs are paid is operating income. The company will have a budget goal for operating income. Value added dollars need to be high enough to pay fixed costs and

The manufacturing company described in Chapter 7 is an example of a company with a profit problem, unrelated to recession. The company, a subsidiary of a large corporation, lost money for three years. Corporate headquarters ordered cost reductions. Losses continued. Then company managers learned the methods and measures of Company P&L Economics. Using these methods and measures they implemented five actions that made the company profitable in six months. Read about this example in Chapter 7.

achieve the budget goal for operating income. Everything relates to everything else. And all can be managed, at the same time, using Company P&L Economics.

## OPERATING INCOME

Operating Income is the focus of Company P&L Economics. Companies using this economics can manage, and, if desired, improve operating income. Operating income is the income earned by the company doing what the company was organized to do. Company people working with the company's capital resources create value in the products and services sold to customers. The company's people and the company's capital resources are the company's fixed costs. Value added dollars must be enough greater than the total of all fixed costs for the company to earn the desired operating income.

To produce the company's desired operating income, Company P&L Economics helps company people manage all the variables:

1. Total sales revenue, and the component parts of total sales revenue
2. Variable costs in total sales revenue and in its component parts
3. Value added dollars in total sales revenue and in its component parts
4. Average value added percent in total sales revenue and in its component parts
5. Total fixed costs

All these variables interact, and in combination produce

6. Operating income

Total sales revenue is an aggregation of major segments of total sales revenue, and a huge number of individual transactions. Aggregation loses information, and huge aggregations lose a huge amount of information. So Company P&L Economics takes one more step, and looks also at segments of total sales revenue. For each major segment, Company P&L Economics measures:

1. Segment sales revenue
2. Segment variable costs
3. Segment value added dollars
4. Segment value added percent

Company P&L Economics does not include fixed costs and operating income for segments of sales revenue since this economics does not allocate fixed costs. Value added is what matters for managing operating income.

Company P&L Economics aims to continuously manage operating income, and to improve operating income when needed. Operating income is what the company earns from doing what the company was organized to do. Operating income is the source of company profit. Operating income plus or minus corporate expenses and revenue, and corporate financial transactions becomes company profit.

All the elements that determine operating income need to be managed: sales revenue, variable costs, value added, fixed costs, new product value added, and timely innovations in products, services, and all business functions. Company P&L Economics offers a new, different, and better information resource for managing all these interacting variables.

The other information resource needed is an intimate knowledge of markets, customers, suppliers, competitors, company operations, and the company's products and services. That is knowledge that company people already have. When they also learn the principles and measures of Company P&L Economics they become capable of effective cost and profit management.

Innovation creates the company's future. In many companies, learning and using Company P&L Economics can be an innovation that will help decision-makers at all levels manage operating income, and improve operating income when desired.

## COMPANY PURPOSE

A business is a very complex, purposeful, probabilistic system. A system, and a business, *is* what it *does*. What every business does can be stated very simply. Every business creates value for customers. Business purpose defines what values in products and services, and what customers. Every business has a purpose. Sometimes the purpose of a business is simply understood from what the company does. Better, the purpose of the business is thought about and spelled out in a business definition, including:

1. Company name
2. Unique value offered (competitive advantage)
3. Products and services offered, now and future
4. Markets and customers served, now and future
5. Key goals

The starting point for company success is the unique value, the competitive advantage that can create company success over a decade or more. This unique value, this competitive advantage, is the most important part of a statement of company purpose.

A currently popular idea tends to limit company performance:

## THE PURPOSE OF THE COMPANY IS TO INCREASE SHAREHOLDER WEALTH

A few years ago a consulting company developed a measure of how company profit performance affects shareholder wealth. They called the measure Economic Value Added (EVA). EVA calculated the company's stock market risk premium, adding this to the current minimum risk long-term bond rate to produce a cost of equity rate. The typical cost of equity rate would be something like double the long-term bond rate. Each reporting period the company would calculate its EVA by subtracting this capital charge from the company's net profit after tax. The capital charge was equity times the EVA-calculated cost of equity rate. If the calculated EVA was positive, the company was creating value for stockholders; jf negative, the company was destroying value for shareholders.

The consulting company developed EVA training programs, including actions a company could take to increase their EVA. EVA grew rapidly in popularity as more and more major corporations used it and reported very impressive results. For several years, EVA swept through corporate America as the new guide to success. Soon, however. many of the EVA company successes began developing profit problems, and EVA died as the measure of company success. However,  EVA continues in use as a measure of the company's performance in managing its capital resources.

EVA was sound in advocating a higher capital cost than required by accounting measures.  Company P&L Economics also increases capital costs.  See Figure 2 in Chapter 5.  EVA, however, was not sound in advocating EVA as the measure of business success.

Business success is much more than one measure of one function. More than fifty years ago Peter Drucker, in his book, *The Practice of Management*, first defined the performance areas that determine every company's success. [1] For today, it's appropriate to make a few changes in wording and add one new area to bring Drucker's list up to date:

1.  Creating and keeping customers (sales revenue)
2.  Quality and productivity
3.  Innovation
4.  Organization capability
5.  Physical and financial resources
6.  Public responsibility
7.  Environmental responsibility
8.  Profitability

For enduring success, companies need to perform well in all of these key performance areas. There are useful performance measures in each of these performance areas. These performance areas, however, are not the starting point. The starting point for company success is the unique idea, the competitive advantage, that can create company success over a decade or more.

In 1998, Google started with two partners and one employee in a garage in Menlo Park, California, with a search engine and a unique idea: to organize the world's information and make it universally available and useful.  In a few years that idea created a multi-billion dollar company.

Purpose is the company's driving force. Key goals might include two and five year sales revenue and profit goals.  Key goals will also include goals in some combination of the eight key performance areas listed above that determine every company's success. Having a purpose, the company can then set goals for the months ahead.

One of the goals will be a sales revenue goal. Sales revenue is the first line on the income statement, and the starting point for profitability. Another important goal will be a profit goal. Profit rewards shareholders through dividends and share appreciation. Profit can reward the company's key people through incentive compensation and bonuses. Profit also serves two important economic needs:

1. Profit provides funds needed for maintaining and further developing the company's present operations.
2. Profit provides funds needed to create the company's future, including:

   Product, service, and technology innovation projects
   Innovations in company management and operations
   Acquisitions, mergers, and divestitures

Profit provides funds for the major "futures" projects that create the company's future. Profit also establishes the credit rating that allows the company to raise additional financing at a reasonable cost. In addition to a profitability goal, goals will be set in some combination of the eight key performance areas that determine every company's success.

Cost is what the company pays for the resources it needs to do what it was organized to do. So cost has many connections. Cost connects with all business functions. All incur costs. What the company does in each of the eight key performance areas incurs costs. What company people do incurs costs. Costs connect with everything.

Dictated cost reductions of X number of employees, or $X cost reductions will have many consequences. Such cost reductions affect company performance in some combination of the key performance areas that determine company success, with unpredictable results.

Company P&L Economics provides methods and measures for managing the key variables that result in operating income. Company decision-makers, having knowledge of the company's operations, markets, and customers, can use this information to find the actions that will improve operating income. Actions will be more in areas of creating value than in cutting costs.

Company P&L Economics focuses on operating income. A company is what it does. And what it does earns operating income. Operating income is the source of company profit. Desired profitability begins with the achievement of desired operating income. Company P&L Economics gives decision-makers the methods and the measures that will help them continuously manage operating income, and improve operating income as needed.

## WHY THIS BOOK?

Companies have been managing their costs through an annual budget process that no longer works. The budget process manages fixed costs by the individual line-item accounts in the company's chart of accounts. The individual accounts have names, but they are not identified as fixed costs. There is no total of all fixed costs—people costs, capital costs, and programmed fixed costs.

Managers do not know and do not manage total fixed costs. The result: in most companies, total fixed costs are unmanaged and uncontrolled. The budget process makes no attempt to manage total fixed costs. And the budget process ignores and does not manage variable costs. In times of rapid change, annual budgets become an ineffective way to manage both fixed costs and variable costs, and income.

Companies need methods and measures for managing costs and income hour-by-hour, day-by-day, week-by-week, month-by-month, continuously, as they do their jobs and change happens. They find those methods and measures in Company P&L Economics.

The author has worked with more than a hundred businesses in sixteen countries, using the methods and measures of Company P&L Economics to deal with profit problems. The people in these companies knew very well their markets, their customers, their suppliers, the competitive situation, and all the details of their company operations. When they learned, also, the methods and measures of Company P&L Economics, they were always able to control costs, and improve their achievement of operating income goals.

Company people use Company P&L Economics concepts and measures daily as decisions are made, actions taken. An operating income statement and the company's income model are reviewed monthly to help in identifying and responding to any developing problems, or opportunities. Company P&L Economics becomes a new and very useful resource for management.

For effectiveness, all decision-makers need to learn about and use the concepts and measures of Company P&L Economics. There has been no single, easy to refer to, reference that will help company people learn and use these concepts and these measures. That reference is needed for successful and continuing management of sales revenue and operating income. This book is that reference.

## IMPORTANT IDEAS IN CHAPTER I
## A NEW MANAGEMENT TECHNOLOGY
## —COMPANY P&L ECONOMICS

1.  Company P&L Economics offers the methods and the measures for managing costs and managing income hour-by-hour, day-by-day, week-by-week, month-by-month, continuously.

2.  Companies typically manage costs separately from everything else. Company P&L Economics concepts and measures manage costs in relation to everything else.

3.  The whole company structure, all the company people, all the company capital investment—land, buildings, machinery and equipment—are there to create value for customers, measured by value added.

4.  Company P&L Economics measures and monitors all these key measures:

    *   Total sales revenue, and the component parts of total sales revenue
    *   Variable costs in total sales revenue and in its component parts
    *   Value added in total sales revenue and in its component parts

- Average value added percent in total sales revenue and in its component parts
- Total fixed costs
- Operating income

All are manageable, using the principles and measures of Company P&L Economics,

5. Operating Income is the focus of Company P&L Economics. Companies using Company P&L Economics will manage costs and income to best achieve desired operating income goals.

6. Companies need to set goals and performance measures in some combination of these eight areas that determine every company's success:

    1. Creating and keeping customers (sales revenue)
    2. Quality and productivity
    3. Innovation
    4. Organization capability
    5. Physical and financial resources
    6. Public responsibility
    7. Environmental responsibility
    8. Profitability

7. Company purpose directs all company actions, stating:

    1. Company name
    2. Unique value offered (competitive advantage)
    3. Products and services offered, now and future
    4. Markets and customers served, now and future
    5. Key goals

8. Company purpose can be stated in a single sentence. Examples;

    1906. The Ford Company will build a car that everyone can buy. (Made Ford the leading car company for two decades)

    1998. Google will organize the world's information and make it easily available to everyone. (Made Google a leading company for 15 years, so far)

# Chapter 2

# Origin and Development of Company
# P&L Economics

More than half a century ago a General Electric scientist, Dr. Zay Jeffries, observed that civilization is a race between the integrating talents of man, and the disintegrating forces of accelerating evolution. [2]  Now, more than fifty years later, complexity, as the measure of Jeffries' accelerating evolution, has multiplied within the company and, even more, in the world outside the company where company success is created. And we have a new measure for this growth in complexity: Moore's Law.

In 1965, Gordon Moore, a cofounder of Intel, presented a paper in which he stated that the number of transistors on a chip had doubled about every two years, and projected that this rate of change would continue for another fifteen years. Forty-one years later, in 2006, still doubling on schedule, the number reached one billion. And now, 2011, the doubling continues. Over the years, this Moore's Law rate of change became a planning standard in the electronics industry. Change happens, faster and faster.

How to manage costs, how to manage revenue, how to manage the value-added in the company revenue to achieve desired operating income is more complex than ever. To simplify this complexity and improve our decisions, we now have Company P&L Economics. This author has worked on profit problems with management groups in companies in sixteen countries. We applied the concepts, methods, and measures of Company P&L Economics in a variety of situations. When the goal was profit improvement, profitability improved. Company P&L Economics structures, organizes, and simplifies the complexities of cost and profit management, and helps managers achieve desired results.

## WHAT IS COMPANY P&L ECONOMICS?

Economics studies the functioning of the total economy. Economics analyzes the economy to discover how it works, and the influences that affect or control how it works. From this information, economics establishes measures of the economy and predicts these measures in various scenarios, under stated assumptions.

In a similar way, "microeconomics" studies elements of the total economy: industries, markets, supply, demand, resources, and other components of the total economy.

Recently there developed a new and narrower economics, the economics of the individual business enterprise. This new economics studies the economic functions of the individual company:

1. What the economic functions are
2. How these economic functions work
3. The influences that affect or control how these functions work
4. Useful measures for managing and controlling these functions

Joel Dean, a professor at Columbia University in the 1940s and 50s, pioneered the development of this new economics, which he called managerial economics. Dean's seminal book, *Managerial Economics,* published in 1951, is a useful reference for the concepts, methods, and measures in this new economics. [3] Managerial economics studies manufacturing costs, the costs incurred in the various functions and transactions of the firm, sales revenue, margins, the interactions and the controlling influences affecting all of these, and establishes measures useful in managing them. Managerial economics has developed further over the years in academia especially for use in the areas of production analysis, pricing analysis, capital budgeting, and risk analysis.

I studied with Joel Dean at the Columbia University Graduate School of Business. After graduating from Columbia, I began my business career working for The General Electric Company, a very well-managed company. I quickly learned two things:

1. Joel Dean's managerial economics is very useful in dealing with any situation involving costs, revenue, or income.

2. None of the managers and decision-makers on matters involving costs or revenue or income knew anything about managerial economics.

What my colleagues did know was accounting concepts, methods, and measures and these were their guides. Accounting measures report what's happening on costs, revenue, and profit. But managers have only their own experience and judgment for decisions on what actions to take to improve unsatisfactory sales revenue or profitability, or actions to exploit high achievement further.

Managerial economics gives managers a rich information resource for managing costs, analyzing sales revenue, examining influences on profitability, analyzing production processes and costs, risk analysis, and evaluating other areas of company operations. The managerial economics dealing with cost and profit management, I call Company P&L Economics. Company P&L Economics concepts, methods, and measures are very easy to learn and apply. They give managers and decision-makers at all levels the information they need to make wise decisions on costs, revenue, and income. Using Company P&L Economics, the little to big decisions made in operations every day, and the big decisions made at planning time or budget time become more effective.

Over my career, I have worked with companies in U.S.A., Canada, Mexico, Colombia, Venezuela, Brazil, Argentina, UK, France, Spain, Belgium, Switzerland, Australia, New Zealand, Philippines, and Japan on revenue, cost, and profit problems. Accounting people in these companies could quickly prepare the Company P&L Economics measures we needed. The data are already in the company's chart of accounts, and product cost data.

# LEARNING ABOUT COMPANY P&L ECONOMICS

A two to three hour seminar session is time enough to communicate the basic concepts, methods, and measures of Company P&L Economics to a group of company people. Usually a session like this is given to people who have been struggling with a profit problem, and struggling unsuccessfully. For most management groups with a profit problem, the typical solution they have is "cost reduction."

Cost reduction, however, is seldom a solution. If there is a profit problem there is a reason, or reasons, for the profit problem. Company P&L Economics will tell us the reasons. And when we understand the reasons, we are part way toward finding a solution. Company P&L Economics will help guide us to that solution. A typical experience learning about and using Company P&L Economics to improve profitability would go something like this:

In the morning of the first day accounting people would prepare:

1. A chart of the 12-month moving total of sales revenue over the last three fiscal years and year to date, to see trend and changes. It's most useful to center the 12-month totals. The 12-month total from January 1 to December 31 is plotted at June 30.

Current year to date, monthly numbers for:

2. Total sales revenue
3. Total variable costs
4. Value added dollars
5. Value added percent (3-month moving average)
6. Total fixed costs (3-month moving average)

To calculate total fixed costs, individual fixed cost accounts can be classified into the three categories of fixed costs: people costs, capital costs, and programmed fixed costs. The total of these three is total fixed costs.

- People Costs: All salary, wage, and benefit costs, and other costs of company people
- Capital Costs: All capital costs as shown in Figure 2
- Programmed Fixed Costs: All sales, general, and administrative costs that are not people costs or capital costs

Fixed cost accounts all have names, but they are not identified as fixed costs. Nor are they identified as people costs, capital costs, or programmed fixed costs. For managing costs and operating income it's essential to know, for each reporting period, the total of fixed costs, and the totals of each of the three components of total fixed costs: people costs, capital costs, and programmed fixed costs.

Usually the variable costs of the sales revenue can't be calculated exactly, but can be calculated/estimated accurately enough using product cost data. Having sales revenue, variable costs, and total fixed costs, value added dollars, average value added percent and breakeven can be calculated:

Sales Revenue – Variable Costs = Value Added

Value Added ÷ Sales Revenue = Average Value Added Percent

Total Fixed Costs ÷ Average Value Added Percent = Breakeven

Also during the morning we would have a "Learning about Company P&L Economics" session of accounting, sales, marketing, research and development, manufacturing, and management people. We would discuss the basic concepts of Company P&L Economics, and its methods and measures.

Then in the afternoon we would begin using the measures developed during the morning. We would prepare an operating income statement in Company P&L Economics accounts and discuss what it tells us. We would prepare an income model and demonstrate the effects of changes in the individual measures in the model. We would begin to discuss an audit of variable costs to find opportunities for improving value added. We would look at the trend of fixed costs and discuss ways of controlling this total. We would discuss possible ways for increasing sales revenue. We would also discuss ways for improving the profitability of sales revenue.

However, profitability is only one of the key performance areas. We would also begin to identify where improvement is needed in any of the key performance areas:

- Creating and keeping customers (sales revenue)
- Quality and productivity
- Innovation
- Organization capability
- Physical and financial resources
- Public responsibility
- Environmental responsibility
- Profitability

Typically, improvement in creating and keeping customers increases sales revenue and brings quickest improvement in profitability. Improvements include:

1. Increasing sales revenue

2. Increasing the profitability of sales revenue by increasing average value added percent.

Company P&L Economics provides the information needed to make these improvements.

Improvement in the key performance areas of quality, productivity, and innovation can improve profitability longer term. The very quickest improvement in profitability comes from the use of Company P&L Economics to improve the profitability of present sales revenue.

In two or three days, work can be under way improving the profitability of existing sales revenue. In these two or three days we could also identify where improvement is needed in any of the other key performance areas. We could then start the task of making these improvements. Listed below are some of the results from this kind of effort:

- A specialty plastics start-up determined the actions needed, and achieved sales and profit objectives for the start-up period.

- A merger of two specialty products companies lost market share, and profits turned into losses. Using Company P&L Economics, profitability sharply improved by controlling fixed costs, improving mix, and increasing sales revenue.

- A commodity products manufacturer controlled fixed costs, targeted mix opportunities, and improved profitability.

- A manufacturer of plating equipment and chemicals increased profitability by controlling fixed costs, increasing sales training, and developing a target customer sales program.

- A chemical producer changed pricing strategy, increased margins, maintained market share and improved profitability.

- Using data in a new way, a division general manager was able, after the tenth day of the month, to forecast reliably what the revenue and income for the month would be, by checking a few key measures.

- A Spanish machinery manufacturer identified changes needed in procurement that changed losses into profits, with no increase in sales revenue.

- An industrial equipment manufacturer in England made pricing decisions that ended losses and made the company profitable.

- An Australian company changed sales strategies, increased revenue, and increased profit.

- A specialty materials business in Brazil determined their response to cut price competition, and with plant productivity improvement and increased marketing expenses increased market share and profitability.

- A machinery and supplies manufacturer and reseller in Argentina operated profitably in a hyper-inflation economy.

- A distributor in France changed their product line management methods, reduced fixed costs, and increased profitability.

- A Latin American producer of decorative laminates limited fixed costs and increased sales revenue with sales training and a target account sales program. They also improved mix to increase average value added percent from 38% to 44%. Profit increased sharply.

In all of these examples, the decision-support information was unknown, and the needed actions unseen until the methods and measures of Company P&L Economics were used. Only in one case, were some company people laid off. Assets were not sold. Traditional cost reduction was not imposed. Instead, Company P&L Economics measures were used to increase value added and the profitability of existing sales, and to control fixed costs and improve mix.

Improvements were often made also in the key performance area of creating and keeping customers. There is always opportunity for improving sales revenue, by:

- Changes in territory assignment
- Training in sales territory management
- Customer sales planning
- Target customer sales programs
- Training in professional salesmanship

What is reported in this book results from the experience of many companies using, and developing further, the concepts, the methods, and the measures of Company P&L Economics. Managers and decision-makers at all levels deal with costs, and many deal with revenue and profit management. They need a discipline that will help them manage costs and revenue effectively. Company P&L Economics, the economics of cost and profit management in the individual business enterprise, is that discipline.

## WHY ECONOMICS?

Managers and decision-makers at all levels know accounting concepts, methods, and measures. Accounting measures will tell them when they have a profit problem. But accounting concepts, methods, and measures provide no information on why or how a profit problem developed, or how the present situation can be improved. With no information resources to help them, decision makers rely on their own experience and knowledge. Increase sales? Cut costs? Wall Street likes layoffs. Hmmm.

Profit problems often happen in times of recession, when sales are more likely to fall than increase. Cut costs? Fixed costs? Some programmed fixed costs could be cut, but there's not much saving there.

Capital costs? Some can be deferred, but little opportunity for cuts. People costs? For most companies these are the biggest fixed costs, and can be cut quickly, and increased again when needed. Layoffs happen. Wall Street applauds. The stock rises.

With layoffs there is cost reduction. What else happens inside the company? We live in a systems world. Everything is connected to everything else. There is no cause and effect. There is event and consequences. One thing we can be sure of is that $1 million or $10 million or $100 million in layoff "savings" will not add $1 million or $10 million or $100 million in profit. There may be some effect on profit, up or down. There may also be effects on quality, productivity, sales revenue, new product development, the condition of fixed capital, organization capability and motivation, community and environmental relations, and profitability. None of these may be measureable. But there may be anecdotal evidence.

Company P&L Economics changes this scenario. The methods and measures of Company P&L Economics continuously measure and track the factors controlling operating income. Changes influencing operating income up or down will be seen six months or more before any change will be apparent in financial reports. Furthermore, there will be information on the kinds of actions needed to keep performance on track toward the desired operating income. Managers using Company P&L Economics measures have the information they need to manage costs and help them achieve desired operating income.

Managing costs and operating income needs more than Company P&L Economics measures alone. Also needed is the knowledge and information known by operations people in all of the key performance areas that determine every company's success:

1. Creating and keeping customers
2. Quality and productivity
3. Innovation
4. Organization capability
5. Physical and financial resources
6. Community relations
7. Environmental responsibility
8. Profitability

Especially needed is the knowledge of company people on customers, market, and competitive situations. Having this knowledge, company people can use Company P&L Economics principles, methods, and measures for the continuing improvement of operating income.

Company P&L Economics provides information on actions needed for dealing with profit problems as these problems are developing. Control actions, of course, have consequences. Company P&L Economics helps decision-makers see and understand likely and possible consequences as actions are being considered. Company P&L Economics helps decision-makers keep the consequences positive.

Company P&L Economics gives managers the information they need on costs, revenue, and how costs and revenue relate to create operating income. Operating income is the source of company profit. Company P&L Economics helps all decision-makers take the actions needed to achieve desired operating income. This book explains how.

## SOME USEFUL IDEAS

The principles, methods, and measures of Company P&L Economics are easy to learn, and easy to apply in the decisions managers make every day. The data needed are already available. All the data needed are in the company's chart of accounts and product cost data. These data are being used to develop accounting measures, and to prepare financial reports. Company P&L Economics, however, uses these data in new and very different ways.

A new business discipline often requires some new ways of looking at things. Here are eight new ways of looking at things that are helpful in using Company P&L Economics.

1.  Everything that matters in business is always in motion. The first thing that matters in business is sales revenue. The purpose of any business is to provide products and services that customers will buy and that will satisfy customer expectations. Revenue from customers is the measure of that success. We budget sales revenue at a fixed number for a specific 12-month fiscal year. That's all that management sees of 12-month sales revenue; the 12-month total for the fiscal year, then the 12-month total for the next fiscal year.

There's very little information in these successive 12-month totals. Total sales revenue, and the various parts of total sales revenue are always in motion, always changing. Company P&L Economics monitors these changes. Company P&L Economics provides a 12-month total every month.

Each month Company P&L Economics monitors and charts four key measures needed for managing sales revenue:

(1)  A 12-month moving total of sales revenue
(2)  The variation in sales revenue from a year ago
These two charts show trends, and changes in trends as these develop. See Figure 13 in Chapter 8.
(3)  12-month moving total of value added dollars in total sales revenue
(4)  3-month moving average of value added percent in total sales revenue

Company P&L Economics also monitors the same four measures for each major segment of total sales revenue. This group of measures and charts provides very useful information for planning and managing sales revenue.

Company P&L Economics also monitors and charts 12-month moving totals of operating income, and 3-month moving average of monthly variation from year ago to show trend and changes as they develop. Company P&L Economics is always aiming for goals ahead, and signaling actions needed to achieve those goals. All that matters is always in motion. Everything interrelates.

2.  For cost and profit management, think trends and changes in trends. Instead of thinking specific numbers for a specific period, think of trends. How are the numbers changing? What is the trend? Is there a trend? Is performance moving toward the desired goal? What's changing? What actions are needed? For cost and profit management, Company P&L Economics helps decision-makers answer these questions.

3.  Business decisions are not right or wrong. Some are better than others. In education we learn right and wrong answers. 7 times 4 is 28. The capital of Brazil is Brasilia. These are right answers.

All other answers are wrong. In business there are usually several possible responses to a problem, all different; none clearly right or wrong. In business we seek good decisions, decisions that will produce a desired result. Company P&L Economics helps decision-makers make good decisions to deal with cost and profit problems.

4. A business is a very complex system. Companies like to analyze. They analyze sales. They analyze costs. They analyze products. They analyze markets. They analyze all the parts, all the elements, all the pieces to find ways to improve each one. But improving the parts may not help. The company is not a collection of parts. The company is a system of parts working together to accomplish a purpose.

Management is a synthesis, designing and structuring the parts to work together to accomplish company goals.

Everything is related to everything else. There is no cause and effect. There is cause, action, or event and consequences rumbling through the system. Cost reduction may or may not improve profitability. Cost reduction (action) has consequences throughout the system. Profit improvement may or may not be one of them. Managers using Company P&L Economics will gain a better understanding of these complex interrelationships. They will find effective ways to control costs and improve profitability.

5. The company needs financial controls to maintain a healthy balance sheet. However, financial controls are not useful or effective for managing company operations. For managing company operations we need to work with the revenue and cost measures in operations.

For revenue measures we need to work with accounting, sales, and marketing on total sales revenue, the major components of total sales revenue, and the revenue from individual transactions. We need to know sales revenue, and the component parts of sales revenue. We also need to know the variable costs and value added for each of these, and for transactions as these are being developed. We need to monitor and manage:

1. average value added percent
2. value added dollars
3. total fixed costs

6.  Accounting numbers are precisely right. Company P&L Economics numbers for a specific product at a specific selling price can be precisely right. However, the totals and aggregates we deal with in Company P&L Economics may only be approximately right, because we may not have precisely right numbers for all the components. Using Company P&L Economics, "approximately right" is good enough for making wise decisions. "Precisely right" is needed for financial reporting. For management decisions, "approximately right" can often be the best available information, and can enable wise decisions. For example, the calculation of total variable costs in total sales revenue for an accounting period will likely not be precisely right. But it will be right enough for managing operating income.

A calculation precisely right, can be misleading. Cost accounting can develop a profit figure for an individual product. Following the prescribed procedure this profit figure is precisely right. But the procedure includes assumptions and the allocation of fixed costs. Allocating fixed costs to individual products loses control of fixed costs, and makes the profit figure very unreliable for decision-making. Bad decisions can then happen.

Managers, looking at these product profit figures, may decide to eliminate unprofitable products. However, with these unprofitable products gone, the fixed costs allocated to them remain, and are now distributed among the remaining products, lowering their profit. Also, the value added dollars from sales of these "unprofitable" products are no longer flowing into the company. Eliminating "unprofitable" products can be very costly.

For product decisions, there is much more to consider than a calculated product profit figure. Company P&L Economics does not calculate a profit figure for a product. But it does calculate the variable costs and the value added for each product and each transaction. Variable costs, selling price, value added, and sales revenue are the information needed for product decisions.

7. What is the best way to allocate fixed costs? Over recent years, much time, effort, and money has been spent in developing better and better ways to allocate fixed costs. The most recent best way is activity based costing (ABC). There is a different and better way. Don't allocate fixed costs. We allocate fixed costs in order to calculate the profitability of individual products. We want the profitability of individual products in order to improve the profitability of the company. If we have a better way to improve the profitability of the company we no longer need to allocate fixed costs. And there is a better way to improve company profitability: Company P&L Economics.

Using Company P&L Economics there is no need to allocate fixed costs. Company P&L Economics controls total fixed costs by mea- suring total fixed costs at each monthly closing, and monitoring the changes in this measure. Companies today don't know what their total fixed costs are. For most companies today, their total fixed costs are un- controlled. Using Company P&L Economics, company people measure and manage total fixed costs in relation to the company's value added that pays these costs.

Another example of finding a better way: During the 1980s American companies were automating their warehouses to make them more ef- ficient. At the same time, in Japan, companies were developing the flow manufacturing of the Toyota Production System, eliminating the need for warehouses. Japan solved the warehouse "cost" problem by eliminating the warehouse. Now, with our traditional management, we spend time and effort and money on the best way to allocate fixed costs. At the same time, here is Company P&L Economics that eliminates the need to allocate fixed costs. Company P&L Economics offers a different and better way to manage profitability.

8. Traditional management says that each of the company's products and services must be profitable, to make the company profitable. Company P&L Economics offers a better way to make the company profitable. Company P&L Economics measures and manages sales revenue, variable costs, value added, and fixed costs to create the desired operating income. Operating income is the source of company profit. Company P&L Economics focuses on operating income and provides

the information decision makers need to manage the variables that determine what the operating income will be.

Important Ideas in Chapter 2

Origin and Development of Company P&L Economics

1.  How to manage costs, how to manage revenue, how to manage the value added in the company revenue to achieve desired operating income is more complex than ever. Company P&L Economics simplifies this complexity, and provides the information decision-makers need to control costs and manage operating income.

2.  Accounting measures report what's happening on costs, revenue, and profit. But managers must rely on their own experience and judgment to decide on what actions to take to improve unsatisfactory profitability, or the actions needed to exploit high achievement further. Company P&L Economics gives managers a rich information resource for dealing with cost and profit problems, and exploiting successes.

3.  Typically, improvement in creating and keeping customers increases sales revenue and brings quickest improvement in profitability. Improvements include:

    (1) Increasing sales revenue
    (2) Improving sales mix
    (3) Increasing the profitability of sales revenue by increasing the average value added percent in the sales revenue
    Company P&L Economics provides the information decision-makers need to make these improvements.

4.  Managers and decision-makers at all levels need a discipline that will help them control costs and manage profitability. Company P&L Economics, the economics of cost and profit management in the individual business enterprise, is that discipline.

5.  Managing costs and operating income needs more than Company P&L Economics concepts, methods, and measures alone. Also needed

is the knowledge of company people on customers, markets, and competitive situations. Having this knowledge, company people can use Company P&L Economics principles, methods, and measures to control costs in relation to cash earned, and manage operating income to achieve desired goals.

6. Control actions have consequences. Company P&L Economics helps decision-makers see and understand likely and possible consequences as actions are being considered. Company P&L Economics helps decision-makers keep the consequences positive.

7. Company P&L Economics is always aiming for goals ahead, and signaling actions needed to achieve those goals. All that matters is always in motion. Everything interrelates. Company P&L Economics provides the measures that tell decision-makers what's happening, and actions needed.

8. Company P&L Economics involves all company people in controlling costs, and managing profitability.

# Chapter 3

# Basic Principles of Company P&L Economics

Company P&L Economics offers new, different, better ways to improve revenue, control costs, and manage operating income. All the methods and measures of Company P&L Economics flow from five basic principles. This chapter presents these five basic principles. Understanding these principles, which are different from conventional thinking, is the first step in learning and applying the methods and measures of Company P&L Economics.

The five principles:

1. Profit comes from operating income.
2. Every cost is either a variable cost or a fixed cost.
3. Sales revenue pays variable costs and earns cash. The cash earned is the value added created by the company.
4. Cost management is managing variable costs product by product, and managing total fixed costs in relation to value added and desired operating income.
5. Company purpose directs everything the company does.

# PRINCIPLE 1. PROFIT COMES FROM OPERATING INCOME

*Principle 1. Profit comes from operating income. Sales revenue is the starting point for operating income. Company P&L Economics helps decision makers manage both the volume of sales revenue and the profitability of sales revenue. Company P&L Economics does not calculate profit figures for products, services, or contracts. Products, services, and contracts incur costs and create value added. Value added percent and value added dollars are key numbers for managing operating income. Company P&L Economics does not allocate fixed costs.*

Conventional Practice

It has become standard practice to calculate the profitability of individual products, services, and transactions. To make these calculations fixed costs are allocated to the individual products, services, and transactions. In a manufacturing company, fixed costs may be a third or more of all costs. In a service company, almost all costs might be fixed costs. How fixed costs are allocated significantly affects the calculated profitability of individual products, services, and transactions.

Great effort has gone into the search for the best way to allocated fixed costs. Over recent years activity based costing, ABC, has become the preferred best method. ABC allocates fixed costs on the basis of company resources used. Calculations become complex and difficult to maintain, but management feels the resulting profitability figures are more reliable.

The reason for all this effort to know the profitability of each product, each service, each transaction is to provide information that will help decision-makers manage the profitability of the company. The assumption is that making the products and services profitable will make the company profitable. And to make the products and services profitable, decision-makers need to know the profitability of the individual products and services.

To calculate the profitability of products, fixed costs have to be allocated to products. Product profitability figures will show some products with high profitability, some with about average profitability, some with low profitability, and often some selling at a loss. To improve profitability, management might then decide to discontinue the loss items and some of the low profit items.

However, if this action is taken the fixed costs in the cost calculations for those products still remain, and must now be distributed to the remaining products, increasing their cost and reducing their profit. And with those products gone, the company no longer receives the value added dollars from their sales. The action for profit improvement turns negative. The decision was based on misleading data. Product profitability figures, however calculated, always mislead.

### A Better Way

Any allocation of fixed costs is inherently faulty, leads to bad decisions, and loses control of fixed costs. Company P&L Economics eliminates the need for product profitability data. Instead of calculating product profitability, which is always misleading, Company P&L Economics uses value added, which is always reliable and useful. Value added is what the company is organized to create. Value added pays fixed costs, and provides operating income.

Company P&L Economics enables decision-makers throughout the company to manage fixed costs in relation to value added. Value added is the amount of cash generated in operations. Value added pays fixed costs, with the balance, if positive, operating income; if negative, operating loss. Company P&L Economics provides information on actions needed to achieve desired operating income. Operating income is what the company earns from what it does. Company P&L Economics helps decision-makers in operations achieve desired operating income. Operating income plus and minus corporate costs, revenue, and financial transactions becomes company profit.

Company P&L Economics is used by accountants, and used by decision-makers at all levels of operations. Accountants like Company P&L Economics because with Company P&L Economics they are giving management information that enables management to make wise decisions. Decision-makers like Company P&L Economics because it gives them a reliable understanding of what's happening in revenue, costs, and operating income. It also gives them a way to anticipate the likely consequences from actions being considered.

The Company P&L Economics measures that determine operating income show changes as changes develop. This information helps decision makers take actions as needed to maintain or improve operating income. Company P&L Economics continuously monitors key measures that alert management on any developing problems, and informs management on developing opportunities.

Company P&L Economics does not calculate a profit figure for a product. But it does give us each product's variable costs incurred, value added percent, and value added dollars earned. The total of all value added dollars is the company's value added. Value added pays company fixed costs. After fixed costs are paid, the remainder is operating income:

Sales Revenue – Variable Costs = Value Added

Value Added – Total Fixed Costs = Operating Income

## PRINCIPLE 2. CLASSIFICATION OF COSTS

*Principle 2. Every cost is either a variable cost or a fixed cost:*

*(1) Variable costs. These are the costs of the purchased products, materials, parts, components, fasteners, adhesives, coatings, energy and whatever else is purchased for producing the company's products or services; or purchased for resale.*

*(2) Fixed costs. Fixed costs are constant costs, month after month, whatever the change in sales revenue or production. Fixed costs are the people costs, capital costs, and programmed fixed costs incurred to create and operate the company. Fixed costs are incurred by management decision and continue until changed by management decision.*

Variable Costs

Company P&L Economics manages variable costs the same way they are managed in conventional cost management. These costs are assigned to the individual products for which they were incurred. Each product is assigned the costs of the purchased materials, parts, components, energy, and whatever else is purchased for the production and delivery of the product or service. For each product, the total of these costs is the variable cost for that product. If one hundred units are sold in an accounting period, the company's variable costs for these one hundred units is one hundred times the unit cost. If one thousand units are sold, the company's variable costs for those sales are one thousand times the unit cost.

Sales revenue is the amount of cash received from the sales of the company's products and services. This cash must first pay the variable costs incurred for those sales. The balance after paying variable costs is value added. The total value added dollars for an accounting period is the amount of cash generated by operations. This cash pays the total fixed costs for the period. Cash remaining after fixed costs are paid is the operating income for the period. When the total value added dollars are insufficient to pay the period's fixed costs, the result is an operating loss.

For a manufacturing company, average value added may be in the range of 35% to 55%. Individual sales transactions may be in a range from about zero to 80% or more. Finding ways to increase average value added percent can be an effective way to improve operating income. A service company might have very little or almost no variable costs. So a service company might have a value added at or near 100%. All, or almost all, of sales revenue is value added. Value added is the measure of value created by the company.

Fixed Costs

Company P&L Economics classifies and measures fixed costs differently from conventional practice. No allocations. Fixed costs are classified, measured, and managed where and when incurred. Where fixed costs are incurred, they are classified and measured in three major categories:

1. People costs
2. Capital costs
3. Programmed fixed costs

The total of people costs, capital costs, programmed fixed costs and the total of all fixed costs are important control measures in Company P&L Economics. In conventional measurement and management of fixed costs, these totals are not measured and not known. The individual fixed cost accounts in the company's chart of accounts all have names. But they are not identified as fixed costs. They are not identified as people costs, or capital costs, or programmed fixed costs. They are not budgeted or controlled as fixed costs, and management never sees the totals of all fixed costs.

Budgeting hundreds and even thousands of fixed cost line item accounts does not manage the totals of all these accounts. The result, in many companies, is that fixed costs over time grow out of control until a profitability crisis forces a restructuring. In companies using Company P&L Economics that will not happen. Using Company P&L Economics enables management to control fixed costs in relation to cash earned and operating income desired. Fixed costs do not grow out of control.

One of the key benefits of Company P&L Economics is that its concepts, methods, and measures enable decision-makers to manage total fixed costs. In most P&L businesses there is no measure of total fixed costs. Hundreds, or thousands, of fixed cost line item accounts are budgeted and controlled, account by account, in the budget process. But there is no budget and there is no control of the total of all fixed costs. Company P&L Economics has a strong focus on total fixed costs, and on each of its three components: people costs, capital costs, and programmed fixed costs. Actions over time include:

1. Limiting fixed costs in relation to value added cash earned, and desired operating income

2. Increasing value added cash earned

Company P&L Economics provides the information needed for both.

## PRINCIPLE 3.  SALES REVENUE, THE SOURCE OF CASH AND PROFIT

*Principle 3. Sales revenue pays variable costs. The margin above variable costs is value added. Value added pays fixed costs for the period. After fixed costs are paid, the balance is the operating income for the period. All companies are organized to create value for customers. Value added is the economic measure of the value created for customers. Value added minus total fixed costs equals operating income.*

Strategic Components of Sales Revenue

There is much more to sales revenue than the total figure. Sales revenue is a total of very important strategic components. These strategic components include products, product lines, distribution channels, markets served, major customers and perhaps other strategic components as well. How the company will deal with each of these components is an important strategic decision. For on-going decisions and actions and for planning ahead, each of these strategic components needs to be measured and monitored in Company P&L Economics accounts. For each of these strategic components, Company P&L Economics measures:

- sales revenue
- variable costs
- value added

Accounting will prepare the numbers; marketing and sales will be the key users. Marketing and sales will use the information to help them continuously improve sales operations, and continuously improve operating income. Improvement will concentrate on increasing sales revenue, and increasing the value added in the sales revenue. This work will involve also production, product engineering, purchasing, and accounting.

Improving the Profitability of Sales Revenue

Sales revenue is the top line on the income statement. Sales revenue is whatever it is. However, sales revenue can be improved in two ways:
(1) by increasing the amount of sales revenue
(2) by increasing the profitability of the sales revenue

Increasing sales revenue increases profitability. There is also the opportunity to increase profitability by increasing the average value added percent in the sales revenue by:

1. Reducing some variable costs

2. Selling more of the high value added products

3. Redesigning or reformulating some products using the principles of value engineering

4. Substituting high value added products for low value added products where possible

5. Selectively raising some prices.

Company P&L Economics helps decision-makers make wise decisions on each of these.

Increasing Sales Revenue

Company P&L Economics can also help marketing and sales people develop plans and programs for increasing sales revenue. Company P&L Economics provides information that helps management structure sales assignments. Company P&L Economics also provides information helping sales people manage their sales assignments for continuous improvement in sales revenue.

When managers learn about Company P&L Economics, they see very quickly how they can use data they already have for controlling costs more effectively, and for managing operating income to achieve desired goals. To improve operating income, they will find opportunities to:

- increase individual product value added
- increase average value added percent
- increase value added dollars
- control total fixed costs
- increase total sales revenue

Company P&L Economics helps marketing and sales people increase sales revenue by providing them useful data on:

- component parts of total sales revenue
- sales to individual customers
  - major customers
  - all others
- individual transactions
- proposals

In addition, Company P&L Economics requires the disciplines of sales management and professional salesmanship.

## PRINCIPLE 4. MANAGING COSTS IN RELATION TO CASH EARNED

*Principle 4. Cost management is managing variable costs and prices to achieve needed value added, and managing fixed costs in relation to value added and desired operating income. Sales revenue pays variable costs. Value added pays fixed costs. Value added minus total fixed costs equals operating income. For each accounting period, these relationships are measured and monitored in a Company P&L Economics operating income statement, and an income model.*

The Company P&L Economics operating income statement and income model include seven key measures:

1. Total sales revenue
2. Variable costs
3. Value added
4. Average value added percent
5. Total fixed costs
6. Break-even
7. Operating income (or loss).

Key Measures

All seven are key Company P&L Economics measures, essential for controlling costs and managing operating income. Executives and managers today see only one of these seven key measures—total sales revenue. They also see a figure for operating income, but the figure they see will be different, because Company P&L Economics has higher capital costs. These seven key measures will enable company people at all levels to control costs in relation to cash earned, and to manage all of these measures to best achieve desired operating income.

In Company P&L Economics the figure for total sales revenue is the same as the accounting figure. The other six are new or different. Companies today don't know the total of their variable costs and their value added. They don't know their average value added percent. They don't know their total fixed costs. They may calculate a break-even. Company P&L Economics calculates the breakeven for each accounting period. Companies do report operating income. The operating income reported by Company P&L Economics accounts will generally be lower, due to its higher capital costs.

Data sources and Reporting

Company P&L Economics uses the company's existing chart of accounts and product cost data. But it uses these data in new and different ways to control costs and manage income. Accountants and decision-makers at all levels can learn Company P&L Economics easily. Within a day they can learn the principles and calculate some of the key measures. They can begin applying Company P&L Economics to control costs and manage profitability.

Companies using Company P&L Economics prepare the operating income statement and income model for each accounting period, and monitor each of the key measures in time series reports and charts. The income statement and income model show the current situation. The time series reports and charts indicate progress toward goals, and when changes are developing. These changes provide information on both developing problems, and developing opportunities. This is new information, not available in conventional reporting. This information improves predictive management. Company P&L Economics improves the reliability of predictions. More reliable predictions means better decisions today.

## PRINCIPLE 5. COMPANY PURPOSE DIRECTS ACTIONS

*Principle 5. Every company exists for a purpose.* Company purpose directs everything the company does. *The company plans, and undertakes, actions and investments to move the company toward the achievement of its purpose. A Statement of company purpose needs to be on the table wherever and whenever decisions are made. Company purpose is always the first consideration in all plans, actions, and investments.*

A company can be described as a viable, very complex, *purposeful*, probabilistic system. "Purposeful" is the company's driving force. In 1906, the purpose of Henry Ford's new car company was to build a car that everyone could buy. In the 1970s, Bill Gates and Paul Allen were writing software to create a useful PC, the MITS Altair, introduced in January, 1975. In another five years they had developed the operating system chosen for the IBM PC, launched in 1981; and Microsoft was born, to make the PC useful. In 1998, the purpose of Sergy Brin's and Larry Page's new "Google" search company was to organize the world's information and make it universally accessible and useful. Purpose determines what matters. Purpose directs everything the company does. Purpose creates great companies.

All decision-makers need to know and clearly understand the purpose of their company. Then, for new plans, new actions, new investments, they first consider company purpose and how important these plans, actions, investments are to the achievement of that purpose.

Evaluating plans, actions, and investments in relation to company purpose is a judgment call for the decision-maker. But knowing that achievement of purpose is the number 1 consideration will inspire good decisions. Then Company P&L Economics can be used to evaluate the effect on sales revenue, variable costs, value added, fixed costs, and operating income. The decision maker puts the plan, the action, the investment on the company's income model to determine and evaluate the changes.

## CONCLUDING COMMENTS

Understand these five basic principles, and Company P&L Economics will be easy to learn and to apply to control costs and manage operating income. Company P&L Economics helps decision makers manage all the variables that determine operating income. Current budget methods do not deal with variable costs. Current budget methods do not control total fixed costs. Company P&L Economics does. And Company P&L Economics helps also in developing plans and programs for the new products, the new ventures, and the innovations that will create the company's future.

# IMPORTANT IDEAS IN CHAPTER 3,
# BASIC PRINCIPLES OF COMPANY P&L ECONOMICS

Chapter 3 presents five basic principles of Company P&L Economics. Understanding these principles, which are different from conventional thinking, is the first step in learning and applying the methods and measures of Company P&L Economics.

The five principles:

1. Profit comes from operating income which is earned by everything the company does in making and selling its products and services.
2. Every cost is either a variable cost or a fixed cost.
3. Sales revenue pays variable costs and earns cash. The cash earned is the value added created by the company.
4. Cost management is managing fixed costs in relation to cash earned.
5. Company purpose directs everything the company does.

# Chapter 4

# Managing Variable Costs to Improve Operating Income

Variable costs are the costs of the materials, parts, components, fasteners, adhesives, coatings, energy, and whatever else is purchased to produce and deliver the company's products and services. For every product made by the company there is a bill of materials listing all the materials, parts, and components needed to produce the product. The company's chart of accounts and product cost records provide all the data needed to calculate the variable costs of each product, and the variable costs for the products sold in an accounting period.

Some service companies, such as a law firm or a consulting firm, may have few if any variable costs. All or almost all of their costs are fixed costs.

## DEFINITION OF VARIABLE COSTS

In Company P&L Economics every cost is either a variable cost or a fixed cost. Every variable cost item goes directly into the production of a company product or service. Typical variable costs include purchased:

- Raw material
- Parts
- Assemblies
- Fasteners
- Adhesives
- Coatings
- Energy
- Packaging material, and
- Whatever else goes into the production and delivery of the product, and
- The cost of products purchased for resale.

All Company P&L Economics variable costs are direct costs, but they differ from the accounting definition of direct costs. Accounting may define production labor as a direct cost, a variable cost. In Company P&L Economics labor is considered a fixed cost. Labor does not vary with production. Labor cost remains unchanged with normal variations in production. Labor cost stays unchanged until there is a management decision to change the number of workers or change workers' compensation and benefits.

The number of people employed by the company and their compensation is a part of the structure of the company and remains the same until changed by management decision. The materials and parts that are used to manufacture the products vary directly with production. The cost of these materials and parts are variable costs. Each time a product is made it uses the same list of materials and parts to produce the product. Variable costs vary directly with production. Fixed costs, including production labor, are determined by management decision. Variable costs are determined by production.

In some situations, labor can be a variable cost. For a general contractor, a subcontractor is a variable cost. For a landscape company hiring labor from a labor pool for a particular job, that labor is a variable cost of that job.

In Company P&L Economics, assigning costs as variable costs or fixed costs is easy to do, and extremely important for cost management. Without knowing variable costs and value added by product and transaction, neither variable costs nor value added can be managed effectively. Few companies use this information, and they make uninformed decisions on cost and profit management.

## REPORTING FOR AN ACCOUNTING PERIOD

Company P&L Economics information will be used hour-by-hour and day-by-day for cost and profit decisions. This new economics uses the same data as accounting, but uses these data in very different ways. The data are used to develop the economics measures needed to control costs and manage operating income. With these new measures and methods, decision makers can steer costs and income to desired goals.

At each month's closing, the management team reviews the Company P&L Economics operating income statement, and operating income model, explained in Chapter 7. They will also review the time series data and charts of key measures. With this information, and the knowledge of present business conditions—markets, customers, competitive situation, economic conditions—appropriate actions can be taken to keep performance on track toward desired goals.

For each accounting period, Company P&L Economics calculates the total variable costs of the products sold during that period. This is a key measure for understanding costs and changes in operating income. But companies today don't know and don't use this measure. Company P&L Economics does calculate this measure and instructs on how to use the measure to manage variable costs and value added. The first step is to monitor total variable costs, value added, and value added percent of sales revenue  in a monthly Company P&L Economics operating income statement.

Knowing the variable costs for an accounting period, the value added dollars and the value added percent of sales revenue for the accounting period can be calculated. Value added is the difference between total variable costs and sales revenue. The value added percent of sales revenue is value added dollars divided by sales revenue. Read about the example in Chapter 7.

In addition to the measure of total variable costs, companies using Company P&L Economics will also examine the variable costs and value added, product by product and transaction by transaction.  Data are available in the company's product cost data, and from purchasing, for making these analyses. While the average value added percent might be 40%, the range might be from about zero to 70% or more. Companies today do not know what these numbers are and what this range is. They don't know the measures. But they can know them, easily, by using the spread sheet format shown in Figure 4. All the data are in the company's chart of accounts and product cost records.

Value added is the cash generated by operations. This is the cash available to pay the company's fixed costs and provide operating income. A key measure needed for cost management is the value added percent—total value added dollars as a percent of sales revenue. For companies using Company P&L Economics, value added percent is one of the key measures in the monthly operating income statement. Value added percent is one of the first measures decision-makers examine to find opportunities for improving operating income.

## AUDITING SALES REVENUE TO INCREASE VALUE ADDED

A fast way to increase operating income is to increase value added percent, by some combination of:

- Increasing sales of high value added products
- Variable cost reductions
- Product redesign or reformulation, using the principles of value engineering
- Selected price increases
- Increasing the value added in large volume, low value added products

An audit of product sales in the most recent accounting period will provide information needed for discovering opportunities for change and improvement in variable costs, prices, and mix. This audit procedure is described and illustrated in Figure 4, Chapter 6.

For a manufacturing company, a product audit may show a range in value added percent in the company's products from near zero to over eighty percent. Typically, the average will be between 35% and 55%. Sales, product engineering, and purchasing people together can look for opportunities for improving value added for products with lower value added than the average. All products will be examined, beginning with higher-volume products. There may be opportunities, too, for improvement in products with above average value added.

Beginning with the higher-volume products, finding practical improvements for individual products will increase operating income:

- On what products can variable costs be reduced without affecting product characteristics?
- On what products can variable costs be reduced, improving desired product characteristics?
- How can we increase sales of high value added products?
- What products can be redesigned or reformulated to increase value added?
- On what products can the price be increased without loss of sales?

An audit provides very useful economic information. But for good decisions on actions for profit improvement additional information is needed. In addition to the economic information, decision-makers need information on customers and the competitive situation in the marketplace. Product decisions need to be good for the customer. Price decisions need to be acceptable to customers. For price increases, the sales people have to be able to sell the price. To improve mix, sales people can work on ways to sell more of the high value added products.

Product development can also contribute to improving average value added percent. For the development of new products, product specifications can include a desired value added percent. Companies using Company P&L Economics will quickly develop a targeted average value added percent needed to achieve the desired operating income. A new product target value added percent could then be this figure, or higher. However, there will be exceptions. A large volume new product with a value added lower than this target might contribute a very satisfactory number of value added dollars. Having the data enables wise decisions.

All the key measures that determine operating income are inter-related. Effects of changes on operating income:

- Sales revenue. More increases operating income, less reduces operating income.
- Average value added percent. Higher increases operating income, lower reduces operating income.
- Total fixed costs. Higher reduces operating income, lower increases operating income.

Company P&L Economics helps decision-makers at all levels manage these measures to achieve the desired operating income. The monthly income model described in Chapter 7, and the trend measures and charts described in Chapter 8, enable decision makers to control costs and manage operating income.

## IMPORTANT IDEAS IN CHAPTER 4, MANAGING VARIABLE COSTS TO IMPROVE OPERATING INCOME

1. In Company P&L Economics every cost is either a variable cost or a fixed cost. Every variable cost item goes directly into the production of a company product or service.

2. To Improve operating income, decision makers need to know variable costs and value added by product and transaction. They also need to know variable costs and value added in sales revenue, and the major segments of sales revenue. Few companies have this information, and they make uninformed decisions on cost and profit management.

3. Average value added percent is one of the first measures to examine to find opportunities for improving operating income.

4. Beginning with the higher-volume products, finding practical answers for these questions on individual products will increase operating income:

- On what products can variable costs be reduced without affecting product characteristics?
- On what products can variable costs be reduced, improving desired product characteristics?
- How can we increase sales of high contribution margin products?
- What products can be redesigned or reformulated to increase value added?
- On what products can the price be increased without loss of sales?

5. Companies using Company P&L Economics will quickly develop a targeted average value added percent needed to achieve the desired operating income. A target value added percent for new products could then be this figure, or higher.

# Chapter 5

# Managing Fixed Costs in Relation to Cash Earned

Fixed costs behave very differently from variable costs. Fixed costs are costs incurred by management decision to establish and operate the company. Fixed costs do not change with increases or decreases in production and sales. Fixed costs are incurred by management decision and remain unchanged until changed by management decision.

## FIXED COSTS

Total fixed costs is a key measure in Company P&L Economics. The totals of each of the three components of total fixed costs are also key measures:

1. Total people costs +
2. Total capital costs +
3. Total programmed fixed costs = Total Fixed Costs

In today's management reporting this information on total fixed costs is not reported. Managers today don't know what their total fixed costs are. In a service business with few or no variable costs (a law firm, an accounting firm) all costs may be fixed costs. In these firms, decision-makers know the fixed costs, line item account by line item account. They do not know the total of all fixed costs and the changes and trend of this total. In every business, monitoring total fixed costs and the changes in total fixed costs is an essential part of managing operating income.

In the company's chart of accounts there are many, many accounts that are fixed cost accounts. Each account has a name, but the accounts are not identified as fixed costs. The accounts appear in the budgets and budgetary control reports for each of the budgeted units of the company. So the total number of these accounts is huge. All these accounts are managed individually, account by account. Management makes decisions account by account, but there is no measure of the total. Managing all the fixed cost accounts individually does not manage the total of all fixed costs.

When a company begins using Company P&L Economics for cost control and profit management, managers do see total fixed costs, and the trend of total fixed costs. What they usually see is that total fixed costs have been uncontrolled in relation to the value added dollars generated from sales revenue to pay these fixed costs, plus provide operating income.

### People Costs

People costs include all wages, salaries, incentive compensation, bonuses, and any other compensation paid to company employees. People costs also include the costs of all employee benefits—health insurance, life insurance, pension/retirement benefits, social events, and the cost of any other employee benefit. People costs also includes the cost of payroll taxes, workman's compensation, and any other employment costs. In most companies, people costs are the major part of fixed costs.

During the 2008-2010 financial recession many companies sharply cut jobs. Wall Street and company financial management urged layoffs as the best and only way to reduce costs and survive. Decisions on layoffs were made at executive levels far removed from the areas impacted by the decision. Had the people costs part of company fixed costs grown out of control? Whether or not people costs were too high, layoffs were the only way to reduce costs significantly, and quickly.

Variable costs can't be cut by management decision. These costs are incurred to make the company's products. These costs go down as sales go down, or as item by item cost reductions can be negotiated with vendors. Capital costs are sunk costs; no opportunity for significant cost reductions there, although new investments can be postponed. Programmed fixed costs can be cut, but no big numbers there. That leaves layoffs as the only source for quick and large reductions in fixed costs.

Cost reduction is one response for dealing with a profit problem. Cost reduction may help. But cost reduction can have harmful consequences, too. Read about the example at the end of Chapter 8. Often more useful are actions that can increase value added. Increasing value added increases profitability with no risk of harmful consequences. Company P&L Economics provides the information needed for managing and improving value added to achieve desired profitability.

Capital Costs

Capital costs are the costs incurred for owning and maintaining and operating the company's capital facilities. The company's capital facilities include land, buildings, machinery, computers and information system equipment and software, cars and vehicles of all kinds, and whatever other capital equipment is owned or leased or otherwise employed by the company.

Company P&L Economics calculates some of these costs differently from the way these costs are calculated using accounting rules. Company P&L Economics is an economics discipline, applying the knowledge and methods of economics to the operations of the individual firm. These concepts and measures are economics concepts and measures. They differ from accounting concepts and measures.

Figure 2 illustrates an economics view of capital costs. Company P&L Economics views capital investment differently from the view of finance and accounting. Finance and accounting view capital assets as a stock—valuing each asset at the time of original purchase. Company P&L Economics views capital assets as a flow—valuing assets to current value over time.

**Figure 2**
**Capital Costs**

| Item | How Measured | |
|---|---|---|
| Working Capital | | |
| 1. Cash: | _____ | Monthly average |
| 2. Accounts Receivable: | _____ | Monthly average |
| 3. Inventory : | _____ | Monthly average |
| 4. Total Working Capital: | _____ | Total lines 1, 2 & 3 |
| 5. Fixed Capital employed: | _____ | All fixed capital employed valued at replacement cost |
| 6. Total Capital: | _____ | Total lines 4 &5 |
| 7. Normal interest charge on Total Capital: | _____ | A company selected rate of return on capital x Total Capital (line6) |
| 8. Depreciation: | _____ | Straight-line depreciation of the replacement value (line 5) |
| Associated Capital Costs | | |
| 9. Property Taxes: | _____ | Property taxes paid or payable for the period. |
| 10. Insurance: | _____ | Property insurance costs paid or payable for the period. |
| 11. Maintenance: | _____ | Maintenance costs for the period. |
| 12. Total Associated Capital Costs: | _____ | Total of lines 9, 10 & 11 |
| 13. Total Capital Costs: | _____ | Total of lines 7, 8 & 12 |

Many of the capital costs listed in Figure 2 are the same as reported in financial reporting. But some are different, and higher:

Item 6. Fixed capital employed. This classification includes all of the company's capital facilities valued at replacement cost. Differing from accounting, Company P&L Economics is not a discipline with calculations exact to the penny. Company P&L Economics measures are often approximate, but realistic and reliable.

Valuation at replacement cost will be calculated by using appropriate indexes, known comparisons, and judgment. Planning professionals and accountants, working together, are quite capable of determining a reliable total of fixed capital employed, valued at replacement cost. Very likely, some of these replacement costs will include additional features and capabilities.

Item 8. Normal interest charge on total capital. Company P&L Economics charges an interest rate on assets used.

Item 8. Depreciation. Company P&L Economics ignores original cost and charges a straight-line depreciation rate on the replacement value of capital employed. This cost continues until total depreciation is equal to replacement cost. Total depreciation is then maintained at this point, changing to match changes in replacement value. This method assures that the cash will be available to replace assets.

These three items, 6, 7, and 8, make the Company P&L Economics calculation of capital costs higher than are capital costs measured by accounting rules.

### Economic Value Added (EVA)

In the 1980s a consulting firm advanced a new measure for valuing capital—economic value added (EVA). The consulting firm stated that companies, using conventional accounting measures, were very much understating their cost of capital, and not providing adequately for these costs. The EVA idea was that a company needed to earn more than its real cost of capital in order to create value for share owners.

EVA used risk theory and methods to calculate the percent return an investor could expect from an investment in a portfolio having the same degree of risk as an investment in the EVA company. This percent return times equity was the company's capital charge. The company's EVA was the company's after-tax profit minus this capital charge. If EVA was positive (profit was more than the real cost of capital), the company was creating value for shareholders. If EVA was negative, the company was destroying value for shareholders. A comprehensive discipline was developed to help companies improve their EVAs.

Major corporations adopted EVA, reporting improved profitability, and EVA swept through corporate America. But after a few more years, EVA companies began developing profitability problems. Interest and use of EVA disappeared. EVA, like Company P&L Economics, rightly emphasized that real capital costs are higher than reported and, not paying these costs, companies over time can be liquidating their assets.

But the management of capital resources is only one of the key performance areas that determine every company's success. All must be managed well for company success. EVA concentrated on only one, physical and financial resources. While not adequate as a single measure of overall company success EVA continues to be useful as a measure of success in the management of the key performance area of physical and financial resources. See Chapter 10 for information on the key performance areas that determine every company's success.

Managing Constant Fixed Costs

In Company P&L Economics, people costs and capital costs, together, are the constant fixed costs of the company. These costs were incurred by management decisions to establish and operate the company. These constant fixed costs continue over time until changed by management decision. Of course there are on-going changes in individual constant fixed cost accounts as management decisions are made on salaries, wages, employment, investment and other items in the company's chart of accounts for constant fixed costs.

Companies using Company P&L Economics will see the results of all these individual decisions on the totals for people costs, capital costs, and programmed fixed costs. They will also see the value added dollars from sales revenue available to pay these costs. They will be able to keep these costs and the income available to pay them in the balance needed to achieve desired operating income.

With this information available monthly, along with the time series charts on the key measures, management can take actions as needed to achieve desired operating income. In most companies today, managers do not see the relationship between total fixed costs and operating income, and do not understand this relationship:

Sales Revenue — Variable Costs = Value Added

Value Added – Total Fixed Costs = Operating Income

With Company P&L Economics, managers do see this relationship, and they understand and manage this relationship. For further information on Company P&L Economics reporting, see Chapter 8.

Programmed Fixed Costs

All fixed costs that are not people costs or capital costs are programmed fixed costs. Most of these costs are not as fixed and as constant as people costs and capital costs. But, like people costs and capital costs, they are all costs incurred by management decision. Programmed fixed costs include all sales, general, and administrative costs that are not people costs or capital costs.

Programmed fixed costs include advertising, promotion, travel and entertainment, telephone and all communication costs that are not people or capital costs, professional services, contract research, dues and subscriptions and all other sales, general, and administrative costs that are not people costs or capital costs.

A decision might be made to spend 5% of sales revenue on advertising and promotion. This decision does not make advertising and promotion variable costs. They are still programmed fixed costs because the costs are incurred by management decision. And management may decide to change the 5% at any time. Advertising clearly does not fit the definition of a variable cost. In Company P&L Economics, all costs are either variable costs or fixed costs.

## TOTAL FIXED COSTS

Total fixed costs is the total of all people costs, all capital costs, and all programmed fixed costs. Conventional management does not manage the totals of these costs. First of all, these accounts are not identified as, or thought of, as fixed costs. They are identified and thought of according to the names of the accounts—payroll, social security tax, commissions, depreciation, property taxes, maintenance, telephone, travel, print advertising, web advertising, promotion, etc., etc. A company, or a company business, might have hundreds, or many hundreds of individual fixed cost accounts, each with a name, but not identified as a fixed cost.

Each individual manager is responsible for managing the accounts in the chart of accounts that apply in the manager's area of responsibility. At budget time each year many managers request increases in some of the accounts. The accounts have their own names: advertising, payroll, professional services, etc., and are not identified as fixed costs. When management agrees that the proposed increases will be good for the company, and cash appears to be available in the new budget, a number of these proposed increases may be accepted.

These increases then become on-going, increased fixed costs for the company. During each budget period, all budget accounts are reviewed, typically with more increased than reduced. So total fixed costs tend to rise over time. No one sees a total of all fixed costs. No one sees the increase. No one thinks about the cash available in the value added in sales revenue to pay these costs and provide desired operating income. The result: in most companies, total fixed costs are unmanaged and uncontrolled. So operating income, also, is unmanaged and uncontrolled.

Figure 3 shows the 3-month moving average of total fixed costs in a manufacturing company. Over a 5-year period total fixed costs increased from 12.4 million dollars a month to over 17 million dollars a month, with individual accounts controlled to budgeted amounts. The total of all fixed costs was not known, and was not controlled in relation to cash available.

By year 5 the company had a profit problem. At that time they learned about Company P&L Economics. For the first time they saw what their total fixed costs were. For the first time they saw what their value added dollars were. In year 6 total fixed costs did not increase, and the company began to improve its profitability.

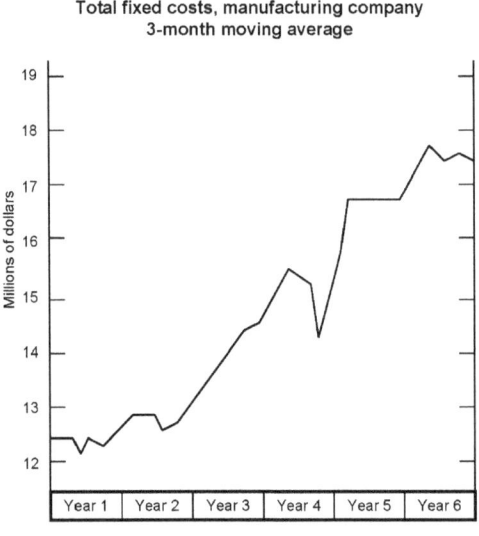

Figure 3
Total fixed costs, manufacturing company
3-month moving average

A large American foods company after learning about Company P&L Economics, calculated their total fixed costs and learned that over the previous five years total fixed costs had increased an average of 15% a year. All fixed cost accounts had been controlled to the budget, but total fixed costs, unseen and unknown, had increased 15% a year!

Over this same five years, sales revenue and the value added dollars in this sales revenue had increased about 5% a year. If management had been using Company P&L Economics over this 5-year period, they would have seen what was happening, and they would have taken corrective actions five years earlier.

Company P&L Economics provides the measures that alert decision makers on any needed corrective action. Key measures include these charts:

1. Total sales revenue: 12-month moving total, centered (12-month calendar year plotted at June 30) See example, Figure 13.
2. Total sales revenue, monthly variation from year ago: 3-month moving average, plotted at middle month. This chart can be combined with the 12-month moving total chart, as shown in Figure 13.
3. Value added dollars: 12-month moving total, centered
4. Value added percent of sales revenue: 3-month moving average, plotted at middle month
5. Total fixed costs: 3-month moving average, plotted at middle month

In addition to charts 1. 2, 3, and 4, on total sales revenue, Company P&L Economics reports these same charts for each major segment of total sales revenue.

To continuously improve average value added percent and value added dollars, there can also be periodic product line audits. These audits determine actions for improving value added product by product, using the spreadsheet format shown in Figure 4.

## CONTROLLING TOTAL FIXED COSTS

To manage fixed costs we need to know more than the individual fixed cost accounts. We need to know, month by month, what the total of all these fixed cost accounts is, and how this total is changing. A simple, and effective way to do this is to construct a 3-month moving average of total fixed costs. The data can be reported. But visuals are better than data alone. In addition to the data, it's helpful to chart the three-month moving total over a period of a few years. Three years is a practical, and useful period, or for whatever period reliable and consistent data are readily available. The 3-month moving average can then be maintained with current data. The 3-month moving average smoothens monthly variations, and over time shows changes and trend.

In conventional cost management, the emphasis is typically on cost reduction. In managing fixed cost there is a different, and more important consideration. We should, of course, always be searching for ways to reduce fixed costs without loss of quality or productivity, or without causing any other undesired consequences. In fact, we are constantly looking for ways to reduce costs and at the same time improve quality and productivity, and other desired consequences.

With fixed costs there is a further consideration. Total fixed costs need to be controlled in relation to the cash generated to pay these costs. This cash comes from the value added dollars in sales revenue. Company P&L Economics provides time series data on total fixed costs and on value added to help management maintain an appropriate relationship between the two, and achieve desired operating income. Value added minus total fixed costs equals operating income.

Conventional reporting reports sales revenue. But conventional reporting does not report the value added dollars in this sales revenue. Company P&L Economics reports the same sales revenue figure. Company P&L Economics also reports the value added dollars in this sales revenue, and the average value added percent of sales revenue. Increasing this average value added percent is often the fastest way to increase operating income.

This value added data is included in the monthly income statement, and income model. The data is also tracked in moving totals and moving averages. This same value added data is also reported and tracked for each of the major segments of total sales revenue.

## IMPORTANT IDEAS IN CHAPTER 5
## MANAGING FIXED COSTS IN RELATION TO CASH EARNED

1. Value Added – Total Fixed Costs = Operating Income

2. Key measures include these charts:

   Total sales revenue: 12-month moving total, centered

   Total sales revenue, monthly variation from year ago: 3-month moving average

   Total fixed costs: 3-month moving average

   Value added dollars: 12-month moving total, centered

   Value added percent: 3-month moving average

3. Total fixed costs is a key measure in Company P&L Economics. The totals of each of the three components of total fixed costs are also key measures:

   Total people costs +

   Total capital costs +

   Total programmed fixed costs = Total Fixed Costs

4. Managers today don't know their total fixed costs. They don't know their total people costs, their total capital costs, their total programmed fixed costs.

5. Company P&L Economics charges a straight-line depreciation rate on the replacement value of capital employed. This cost continues until total depreciation is equal to replacement cost. Total depreciation is then maintained at this point, changing to match changes in replacement value. This method assures that the cash will be available to replace assets.

6. Managers using Company P&L Economics will see the value added dollars in sales revenue. These value added dollars pay all fixed costs and provide operating income. Managers will be able to keep total fixed costs, and the income available to pay these costs, in the balance needed to achieve desired operating income.

7. In the conventional budget process, total fixed costs are unknown and unmanaged and tend to rise over time. Also unknown and unmanaged is the cash available in value added to pay these costs and provide desired operating incotme. Company P&L Economics provides time series data on total fixed costs and on value added to help management maintain an appropriate relationship between the two.

# Chapter 6

# Managing Sales Revenue for Continuous Improvement

The common view is that sales revenue is whatever the sales force delivers. But what the sales force delivers can often be improved, in four important ways:

1. More sales
2. More operating income from existing sales
3. New product sales
4. New venture sales

In sales, and in other areas, too, there is always opportunity for change and improvement. In sales, change and improvement begins with an understanding of present customers, and prospective customers. This understanding can begin with an audit done by sales people. They know the customers and can see where there are opportunities. This audit can't be done by the numbers alone. In addition to "what is," there is always the question of "what can be." Sales people can see both "what is" and "what can be." "What can be" requires a broad knowledge of customer situations, markets, and competitive activity.

## FINDING OPPORTUNITY FOR ADDITIONAL SALES REVENUE

The search for opportunity begins with analysis. For each sales area, the salesperson can list all present customers with sales revenue last two years and current year-to-date. Then apply the 80/20 rule—something like 80% of sales revenue will come from about 20% of the customers. The 80/20 rule is a generalized rule of concentration that applies broadly, in everything. In sales, the few that account for most of the sales are the company's major customers. These major customers get concentrated attention and development.

The relationship with each major customer becomes more a partnership than simply a seller- buyer relationship. Sales transactions become relationships that benefit both parties. Key people in the company know their counterparts in the customer company, and they collaborate, as appropriate. The sales contact person works as a quarterback, bringing company capability to the customer to satisfy customer needs.

A customer audit becomes a search for opportunity. The audit will answer the following questions:

- What is most important to customers in their purchase decisions?
- What are the company's strengths and weaknesses in what matters most to customers?
- How can we increase sales to present major customers?
- Who could be a major customer, but isn't?
- What prospective new customers can be identified?
- Which of these prospective new customers could become major customers?

Identifying what customers value, as illustrated in Figure 6, can be an important part of this audit. This kind of a customer and prospect audit by salespeople will always find opportunity for additional sales revenue.

## MANAGING THE CASH EARNED IN SALES REVENUE.

In our personal lives, in our households, we manage costs in relation to income available to pay those costs. In our business lives, in our companies, conventional management thinks cost management means cost reduction. In business we do want everyone to be searching for ways to reduce or eliminate cost without harmful consequences; better yet, with a benefit. A cost reduction, for example, might also prevent error, or increase capacity. However, there is much more to cost management than cost reduction.

In business, like in our household, there is also the constraint of relating costs to the available cash income to pay both variable costs and fixed costs. Variable costs are paid by sales revenue. Fixed costs are paid by the value added in sales revenue. So cost management is primarily concerned with fixed costs. Company P&L Economics continuously relates fixed costs to the cash available in value added to pay these costs. The cash available comes from sales revenue. But not all the cash from sales revenue is available.

The cash from sales revenue must first pay the variable costs incurred to produce the products sold. And variable costs must be paid with enough cash remaining to pay all fixed costs and provide the desired operating income. After variable costs are paid, the remainder is value added. This value added is the cash available to pay fixed costs. After fixed costs are paid, the balance, if positive, is operating income; if negative, operating loss:

Sales Revenue – Variable Costs = Value Added

Value Added – Total Fixed Costs = Operating Income

Sales revenue is a huge total of all the sales made by the company during an accounting period: month, quarter, year. Like all totals, the sales revenue total loses a lot of information. Each market sold to will have unique marketing characteristics. Different products might be sold to different markets. Each product/market segment will have unique marketing characteristics. There may be more than one channel of distribution (direct to end user, to end users through distributors, to end users through retailers through distributors, to end users through retailers sold directly, etc.) Each channel will have its unique marketing characteristics.

Depending on how sales assignments are made, there may be unique differences by sales assignment. Following the Pareto principle of concentration, about 80% of sales revenue will come from about 20% of the customers. That 20% need to be managed as major customers to assure sales continue and, as possible, increase.

Managing sales revenue requires information on all the strategic components of total sales revenue. Strategic components might be channels of distribution, markets, or products or product groups, or product/market segments. Determining the strategic components, developing the data, and deciding on appropriate actions requires the collaboration of sales, production, accounting, purchasing, and others.

The management of sales revenue becomes an important part of cost management. Cash comes from sales revenue. Costs have to be managed in relation to cash available to pay the costs. Company P&L Economics provides the information needed by decision makers for managing this relationship successfully.

Sales revenue can increase cash available for paying costs, and adding to operating income, in two ways:

1. By increasing the value added in existing sales revenue
2. By increasing sales revenue

## INCREASING VALUE ADDED IN EXISTING SALES

Business people tend to consider that sales revenue is whatever it is, and cash available is whatever it is. New opportunities appear when we discover that both sales revenue and cash available from sales revenue are manageable. Company P&L Economics measures sales revenue and the variables that determine the cash available from sales revenue. Company P&L Economics provides the following data, which is needed to manage both sales revenue and the cash available from sales revenue:

1. Total sales revenue
2. Variable costs
3. Value added
4. Average value added percent

Company P&L Economics also reports the above information on each of the strategic components of total sales revenue, typically channels of distribution, major products and product lines, and markets.

Every sale of a product or service produces value added. The value added is the cash available from that sale after paying the variable costs incurred to produce the product or service sold. The total cash received from the sale is sales revenue. But only part of that sales revenue—value added— is cash available for paying fixed costs and contributing to operating income. Managers using Company P&L Economics will continuously search for ways to increase value added.

The average value added percent for an accounting period can be increased in four ways:

1. Negotiate price reductions on individual variable costs
2. Improve mix by increasing sales of higher value added products
3. Redesign or reformulate some products to increase value added
4. Increase some prices

A good way to discover opportunities for improving value added is to audit all products to determine the value added for each product at the present selling price and present variable costs. Figure 4 illustrates an audit procedure.

**Figure 4**
**Product line audit spreadsheet**

Prepaired by:_____    Product line:_____

Date:_____    Market Growth Rate (1)_____

Period:_____    Competitive Position (2)_____

| Products | Units Total 1 | $ Total 2 | Unit VC 3 | Tot VC 4 | VA $ 5 | VA % 6 | Average SP/Unit 7 | Current SP/Unit 8 | Action 9 |
|---|---|---|---|---|---|---|---|---|---|
| P1: | _____ | _____ | _____ | _____ | _____ | _____ | _____ | _____ | _____ |
| P2: | _____ | _____ | _____ | _____ | _____ | _____ | _____ | _____ | _____ |
| P3: | _____ | _____ | _____ | _____ | _____ | _____ | _____ | _____ | _____ |
| P4: | _____ | _____ | _____ | _____ | _____ | _____ | _____ | _____ | _____ |
| P5: | _____ | _____ | _____ | _____ | _____ | _____ | _____ | _____ | _____ |
| P6: | _____ | _____ | _____ | _____ | _____ | _____ | _____ | _____ | _____ |
| P7: | _____ | _____ | _____ | _____ | _____ | _____ | _____ | _____ | _____ |
| P8: | _____ | _____ | _____ | _____ | _____ | _____ | _____ | _____ | _____ |
| P9: | _____ | _____ | _____ | _____ | _____ | _____ | _____ | _____ | _____ |

Total col #2: _____    Tot col #5:_____    Average VA %:_____

(1) Indicate: High-growth over 8% per year. Medium-growth 3-8% per year. Low-growth under 3%per Year. Neg-negative growth rate. Note: all growth rates are in real terms, units or constant dollars.
(2) Indicate Company position among all competitors. Example: 2/10=Company is number 2 of 10 competitors in sales volume for this product line.
Key: VA-Value added, SP-Selling Price, VC-Variable Costs

After completing the information at the beginning of the audit, assemble and calculate the data:

Col. 1. List the unit sales for each product.

Col. 2. List the sales revenue for each product.

Col. 3. List the variable costs incurred for one unit of each product. The variable costs are the costs of the materials, parts, and whatever else was purchased and used to produce the product. The best cost to use is replenishment cost, since the sale of the product must provide funds for replenishing the variable cost item. Purchasing can supply replenishment costs. Or, for an approximation, if using accounting information, LIFO cost might be used as good enough.

Col. 4. Calculate the total variable costs for each product for the period, Col. 1 X Col. 3.

Col. 5. Calculate the value added dollars for each product, Col. 2 minus Col. 4.

Col. 6. Calculate the value added percent for each product, Col. 5 divided by Col. 2

Col. 7. Calculate the average selling price for each unit, Col. 2 divided by Col. I

Col. 8. List the current selling price for each product.

Col. 9. Note actions needed

By totaling columns 2 and 5, the average value added percent can be calculated.

Seeing these data in a spreadsheet provides some very useful information:

1.  The range of sales revenue. Some products sell in much greater volume than others. Some sell in very low volume. This information was generally known before. Here it is seen specifically.

2.  The range in value added percent. For a manufacturing company this range may be from close to zero to eighty percent or more. For a manufacturing company, the average value added percent will likely be between 35 and 55 percent. For a service company with few if any variable costs the value added may be at or near 100%. Value added percent is a manageable measure in Company P&L Economics. Each reporting period a Company P&L Economics operating income statement will include this figure. See Chapter 7.

3.  The range in value added dollars. Value added dollars pay the company's fixed costs. After the fixed costs are paid, the rest of the value added dollars are the company's operating income. Company P&L Economics focuses on operating income. Operating income is what the company earns from what it does. The company produces and sells its products and services to its customers. That's what the company was organized to do. And it has to do this in a way that will produce a desired operating income. Operating income is the source of company profit.

4.  Opportunities for improvement. Examine high volume products with low value added percent. Can value added percent be increased? Examine high volume products with high value added percent. Can more of these products be sold? Examine products with very low value added. Can the value added be increased? Where can a high value added product be substituted for a low value added product? There will be opportunities to improve the value added in some products. There will be opportunities to improve mix.

A product audit like this gives company people the information they need to begin the search for actions to improve value added percent and value added dollars, product by product. The options:

1. Find ways to reduce variable costs
2. Increase some prices
3. Improve mix by selling more of the high value added products
4. Redesign or reformulate some products using the principles of value engineering
5. Increase sales of high value added products

A product line audit will be done by sales people working with accounting and purchasing people. These people need to be trained in Company P&L Economics before working on the audit. A 3-hour training session is usually sufficient. They learn more as they work with the ideas, methods, and measures.

The audit will identify problem products—low sales, or low value added. The audit will also identify opportunity products—high sales, or high value added. An immediate opportunity might then be to improve the sales mix by selling more of the opportunity products. At the same time, problem products might be fixed to become more successful products by reducing variable costs, redesigning or reformulating the product to increase value added, increasing price, or perhaps substituting a higher value added product.

To determine appropriate actions, problem products and opportunity products can be further evaluated using a Product Evaluation and Plan as illustrated in Figure 5. This evaluation and plan information can be prepared by a product manager or a sales person with the help of the appropriate accounting, purchasing, and product development people.

Figure 5
Product Evaluation and Plan

Product:_____
Evaluated by:_____        Date:_____

Year-to-date data for ____months ending_____
Current data:

Sales revenue $_____       Selling price: $_____

Unit sales_____       Variable costs, list:

Av. SP per unit $_____     Items         Cost

Variable Costs: $_____     1._____    _____

Value Added $_____      2._____    _____

Av. Value Added Percent: _____%    3._____    _____

                                4._____    _____

Major Customers for

 this product, list:

1.                            5._____    _____

2.                            6._____    _____

3.                            7._____    _____

4.                            8._____    _____

5.                            9._____    _____

                              10._____    _____

                   Total Variable Cost _____

Major Competitors:      Value added Dollars $ _____

1.                    Value added Percent        _____%

3.

4.

Action Plan:

Action Plan for a Problem Product

From the above data, and with the additional knowledge that sales people have on customers and the competitive situation, a plan can be developed, considering:

    Can we reduce any of the variable costs? What? How?

    How could we redesign the product to increase value added?

    Can we substitute a higher value added product?

    Can we increase price without losing sales revenue?

    What price would customers accept?

    How will we sell the price?

    Action plan:

    Action Plan for an Opportunity Product

From the above data, and with the additional knowledge that sales people have on customers and the competitive situation, a plan can be developed, considering:

    How can we sell more of this product?

Who are the target customers?
What sales aids might be useful in selling this product?
Action plan:

———————————

In working on a product line audit, and working on individual product evaluations and plans, sales people are involved in cost and profit management. Previously, sales people were asked only to manage their sales assignment to achieve a sales revenue goal. In that sales revenue there are costs and value added that determine profitability. Sales people can learn about Company P&L Economics, and can be asked to manage their sales assignments for both sales revenue and value added. And both sales revenue and value added can be a part of the incentive compensation plan.

## INCREASING SALES REVENUE

Company P&L Economics information helps decision-makers, but more information is needed. Also needed is information about the markets and the customers, and information about the competitive situation. Sales people have this needed information. So sales people need to be involved in developing and using the Company P&L Economics information.

The purpose of the company is to create and keep customers. The customers decide what they will buy and where they will buy it. And those decisions are a matter of the value offered to the customers, and the skills of the sales people. What matters to customers in making their purchasing decisions? Figure 6 lists some of the things typically considered in a purchase decision.

Figure 6
What Customers Value

On-time, in-spec delivery
Product meets expectations
Product design

Product quality
Product features
Cost reduction from using the product
Revenue increase from using the product
Price
Cost—price plus in-use cost
Prompt and satisfying response from salesperson
Prompt and satisfying response from service person
New product development
Technical service support
Problem solving
Sales relationship
Reliability of the product
Reliability of the company
Information resource

Price is always a major consideration, but price can vary depending on perceived value. The purpose of a watch is to tell time. Accurate watches sell for $20 or less; and for $5 thousand dollars and more. Any automobile will take you from where you are to where you want to go. A new automobile can sell for less than $20 thousand, or more than $50 thousand. Whatever the price of the watch or the automobile, the customer receives desired value. Values other than price matter. Companies can strive to differentiate their products and sell at higher prices, increasing value added. But at higher prices, the number of sales goes down. From low price, the demand curve usually drops rapidly as price increases. One of the company's strategy decisions is where they decide to compete on the price curve.

Henry Ford, in 1906, aimed to make a car that everyone could buy. He invented the assembly line, designed his cars for the assembly line, manufactured the cars at low cost, and sold them at one-third the price of other cars. Ford quickly became the leading car company, and maintained that position for two decades.

In 2010, at a price of $629, Apple launched its new iPad with a new generation of e-reading, web browsing, search, media watching, and game playing, including video, animation, color, and full screen touch. Apple aims to offer new and attractive values at acceptably high prices.

A year later they announced a new and better iPad, the iPad2, just as competitors were launching their tablets competing with the iPad 1. Apple applies a Moore's Law kind of time scale in developing their innovations. With the new iPad2, they offered a next generation product in only one year. Product designers often aim for a unique design that can then be sold at a higher price. The high value added makes the product a quick success, with increasing success as sales grow.

Larry Page and Sergey Brin, in launching Google, had no need to consider manufacturing cost. The new and better search engine they invented was available to everyone. The internet is free. With no variable costs, value added was about 100%. They had only to manage fixed costs in relation to cash available from investment funding and sales revenue. They concentrated on value that could be provided to customers. What they offered was the world's information, organized and universally accessible and useful. To this resource they connected advertising and other billable services.

Managing sales revenue begins with value offered to customers. An audit of the company's present situation can be helpful in finding opportunity for increasing existing sales, and opportunity for improving values offered. Figure 7 shows a  format for comparing the company's products with major competitors on product and service values to customers.

The table in Figure 7 can be filled in for a product, a product group, or a product/market segment. List on the left all the considerations that matter to the customer in the purchase decision. List the three major competitors in this product/market business. For each customer value listed, in the four squares on the right, rank from 1 to 4 the company and each of the three competitors, 1 best, 2, second best, 3, third best, and 4 weakest. Then, thinking as a typical customer, go down the listing of values and ratings and put a circle around the 1 ratings for those values most important to you as a customer.  Put a double circle around the three most important values. Appraise the company position and take actions as appropriate.

A good way to use this form and this procedure is with a group of sales people, in a session like a brainstorming session with a leader/facilitator. The group, together, works out their responses. This information can be used by sales people in planning their sales calls, and in their interactions with customers and prospective customers. Sales call experience increases our learning and makes this information more and more useful. This information will also help sales management, marketing, product development, and other company people identify opportunities for change and improvement.

**Figure 7**
**Evaluation of competitive position**

Product/Market Business Segment:_____
What is value to the customer?

| List of Values | Co | C1 | C2 | C3 |
|---|---|---|---|---|
| 1 | | | | |
| 2 | | | | |
| 3 | | | | |
| 4 | | | | |
| 5 | | | | |
| 6 | | | | |
| 7 | | | | |
| 8 | | | | |
| 9 | | | | |
| 10 | | | | |
| 11 | | | | |
| 12 | | | | |
| 13 | | | | |

Directions for this evaluation:
1. Under "List of Values" list what is important to customer in making their purchase decision. This list can best be prepared by consolidating and editing the listings of several sales people.
2. List the three major competitors in this product/market business.
    C1:_____
    C2:_____
    C3:_____
3. Evaluation:
Step1. For each customer value listed, rank from 1 to 4 your company (Co.) and each of the three major competitors (C1,C2,C3)-1, best; 2 ,second best; 3, third best; 4,weakest.
Step 2. Now think of yourself as a typical major customer in this product/market business. Go down the listing of values and ratings and put a circle around the 1 ratings for those values most important to you as a customer.
Step 3. Appraise company position and take actions as appropriate.

This form can be completed by the combined work of several sales and marketing people. The audit will provide information on customer values to emphasize in sales, advertising, and promotion, and areas where change and improvement may be needed. The aim is for the company to be number 1 in values most important to the customer.

### Effective Salesmanship

Professional salespeople "counsel with" more than "sell to" their customers. They learn the customer's interests, needs, and concerns in relation to the product or service the salesperson is selling. They learn the competitive situation. Much of the sales call might be asking questions and listening to the answer; often an answer leading to the next question. The professional salesperson asks questions beginning with the words who, how, what, why, where, and when. These are questions that can't be answered with a yes or no. They require a more in-depth answer, and the salesperson learns more information.

This kind of talking-together selling is called "consultative selling." Instead of "selling-to" the customer, the professional salesperson is consulting with the customer. Both learn. Both benefit. This consultative selling process is illustrated in Figure 8.

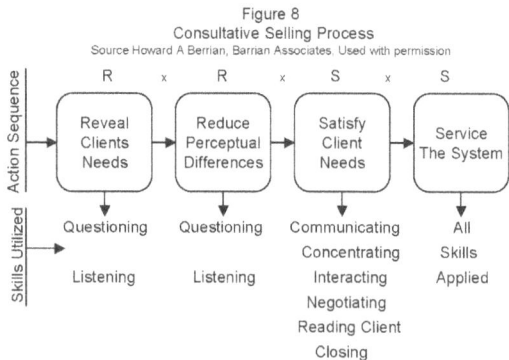

Figure 8
Consultative Selling Process
Source Howard A Berrian, Barrian Associates. Used with permission

The first part of consultative selling, the first, "R," is to reveal customer needs. Professional salespeople aim to satisfy their customers' needs with the products and services offered by their company. So the first task is to learn and understand the customer's needs, interests, concerns, desires, problems, and experience with the product or service being discussed. This is mostly a question and listening discussion with the salesperson conveying an attitude of helpfulness.

The next step the second "R," is reducing perceptual differences. Professional salespeople are experts on the products and services offered by their company. The customer may have only a general impression. However, the customer knows very well all the details of their company's needs and experience with the product and service. In consultative selling and buying, sales representatives need a thorough understanding of the customer situation. The customer needs a thorough understanding of the salesperson's company, products, and services, and what the salesperson can do for them. In this discussion, each party gains a good understanding of the other.

The next step, the first "S," is satisfying the customer's needs and expectations. In this step the professional salesperson offers the company's products and services as an attractive solution to the customer's needs and desires. This is a negotiating session, matching the company's products and services to the customer's situation. In this step, the salesperson asks for and gets the order.

The fourth step, the second "S," the salesperson and others in the salesperson's company service the sale and the customer. The salesperson and the salesperson's company assure customer satisfaction and delight with all aspects of the purchase transaction, including delivery, and whatever further assistance may be needed in the customer's experience with the product and service.

With training and experience, salespeople can become expert in consultative selling. Sales training and experience develops additional skills, too. Professional sales people:

1. Manage the sales assignment as a business
2. Identify major customers and prospects. These are the high-potential customers that will produce about 80% of the sales revenue
3. Concentrate on major customers and major prospects
4. Plan effective coverage of all customers and prospects in the sales assignment
5. Develop action plans for major customers and major prospects
6. Schedule calls
7. Prepare for each sales call
8. See the right people
9. "Counsel with" more than "sell to"

10. Ask questions, listen, ask another question. Ask questions beginning with the words who, how, what, where, why, and when. These are questions that can't be answered yes or no; they require informative answers
11. Maximize face-to-face selling time with customers and prospects
12. Develop proposals good for the customer and good for the company
13. Get the order
14. Follow up and assure that the customer is satisfied, even delighted

With training and experience all of these skills can be learned and further developed.


## AVERAGE VALUE ADDED PERCENT

Sales revenue pays the variable costs of those sales. After the variable costs are paid, the balance is value added. Value added divided by sales revenue is the average value added percent. Each month the Company P&L Economics operating income statement shows total value added dollars, and the average value added percent.

Individual products and transactions will have a range of value added percents. In a manufacturing business, it is not unusual to find some value added percents near zero. On the high side there may be value added percents around 80 percent or more. The average for a successful manufacturing company is usually more than 40 percent. In a service business with few or no variable costs, the average might be at or near 100 percent. This average value added percent determines breakeven. Total fixed costs divided by average value added percent equals breakeven:

$$BE = \frac{FC}{VA\%}$$

BE -- Breakeven
FC – Total Fixed Costs
VA% -- Value Added Percent

Finding actions that will increase the average value added percent will reduce breakeven and improve operating income. Companies using Company P&L Economics have the information they need to increase the average value added percent and improve operating income. The information comes from an audit of products and transactions to learn what was not known before—product and transaction value added. Having this information, opportunities can be found for improvement.

Figure 4 lays out a plan for a product line audit. This is an easy audit to do. All the data needed are already available in the accounting record and in the purchasing department. The audit should be done by sales, accounting, and purchasing working together. The result will be new information that can help decision-makers improve average value added percent. There are 4 ways to increase the average value added percent:

1. Sell more of the high value added products. This becomes a sales project, and involves sales people in two dimensions of sales revenue—increasing sales volume, and increasing the value added in the sales revenue. Some companies using Company P&L Economics have included both sales revenue and value added in their sales reports. They have also included value added in their incentive compensation plans. Company P&L Economics opens many opportunities for change and improvement.

2. Increase the value added in high volume, low value added products. Value added can be improved by:
   Variable cost price reduction
   Reformulation or redesign, using the principles of value engineering
   Replacing with a higher contribution margin product
   Raising price

3. Look throughout the product listing for opportunities to raise price without losing sales. This will be a project of sales, marketing, and general management.

4. Develop new products with higher than average value added. This becomes a collaborative project for sales, product development, purchasing, and whoever else needs to be involved.

When actions are taken on any of these four points, the regular reporting of Company P&L Economics provides the information showing to what extent the anticipated result happens. This is one of the special benefits of Company P&L Economics. Using Company P&L Economics, when actions are taken specific goals can be set. Then the regular reporting will help those involved achieve the goal. Company P&L Economics measures are not used for evaluating performance. They are used to help company people achieve desired goals.

With the product audit information, and the experience of the individuals using the audit, many opportunities for improvement will be discovered. The manufacturing company reported in Figures 9, 10, and 11 after auditing their product line using the method shown in Figure 4, succeeded in finding ways to increase value added. Six months later the average value added percent had increased from 36% to more than 40%. Knowing the numbers, and knowing what needs to be done to improve the numbers, and how to do it, people will find opportunities for improvement.

## TOTAL FIXED COSTS

Total fixed costs are the people costs, the capital costs, and the programmed fixed costs incurred to establish and operate the company. The costs were incurred by management decision, and continue until changed by management decision. In most companies, in most business units in large corporations, managers and decision makers do not know what their company's or business unit's total fixed costs are. Fixed costs include all people costs, all capital costs, and all programmed fixed costs. There are many, many fixed cost line item accounts in every company's chart of accounts. And these accounts appear in all the company's many individual budgets. All the accounts have names, but are not identified as fixed costs. A small company might have hundreds of fixed cost line item accounts. A large corporation might have thousands.

All of these accounts have names, but none are identified as people costs, capital costs, or programmed fixed costs. Managers and decision makers know all about hundreds and thousands of fixed cost line item accounts individually, by whatever their names may be. But they do not know the total of people costs, capital costs, and programmed fixed costs. At budget time, budget figures are proposed by the responsible managers for each of their line item accounts. These proposals are reviewed and finally set by the company's review and approval procedures. Costs are then controlled to the budgets for each line item account.

Since managers often propose increases, and since increases may be approved for some fixed cost accounts, the total of all fixed costs tends to rise. And fixed costs, once incurred, continue until changed by management decision. The key question is not the absolute measure of total fixed costs, but how are total fixed costs changing in relation to cash generation. Cash generation is the value added in sales revenue.

Sales Revenue − Variable Costs = Value Added

Value Added − Fixed Costs = Operating Income

Value added pays fixed costs and must provide also the desired operating income. Company P&L Economics measures this relationship. Company P&L Economics measures total fixed costs. Company P&L Economics measures value added. Value added is the cash available from operations to pay fixed costs and provide operating income.

Conventional reporting does not report total fixed costs. Conventional reporting does not report value added. Conventional reporting does not give management the information needed to manage fixed costs, or operating income. Company P&L Economics does. Company P&L Economics reports both total fixed costs and value added dollars in its operating income statement, as illustrated in Figure 10.

Monitoring this information enables management to consider appropriate actions. In addition to the economics data, management and other decision makers must also consider customer situations, market conditions, and the competitive situation. Actions for improving operating income might include some combination of improving value added, improving mix, increasing sales revenue, new product sales, new business, reducing fixed costs, or increasing some prices.

## OPERATING INCOME

The company's operating income figure is the company's most important, most significant, profit figure. A company *is* what it *does*. And what the company does is produce, sell, and deliver its products and services to customers. The sales of the company's products and services earns the value added that pays fixed costs and provides operating income.

Operating income is where company profit comes from. There may be corporate costs subtracted from operating income. There may be corporate income and financial transactions that add to or subtract from operating income, and increase or decrease company profit. Whatever the corporate transactions, up or down, the source of company profit is operating income. Operating income is what the company earns from what the company is organized to do.

Company P&L Economics gives decision makers the information they need to manage the four variables that determine operating income:

1. Sales revenue
2. Value added dollars
3. Average value added percent
4. Total fixed costs

Company people have always had the figure for total sales revenue. That's the top line on the income statement. With Company P&L Economics, we manage sales revenue using the principles and methods described in this Chapter. We also manage the value added dollars in sales revenue, and the average value added percent. In addition, we manage the value added dollars, and the average value added percent for each of the major segments of total sales revenue.

Many company people are involved in achieving the desired operating income. Sales people are the front line. They get the orders. Each order brings a value added. The professional salesperson brings in the desired sales revenue, and also the desired value added. Companies using Company P&L Economics can give their salespeople responsibility for both sales revenue and value added.

# TEN IMPORTANT IDEAS IN CHAPTER 6 MANAGING SALES REVENUE FOR CONTINUOUS IMPROVEMENT

1. The economics of the business can be expressed in two simple formulas:

   Sales Revenue – Variable Costs = Value Added

   Value Added – Fixed Costs = Operating Income

2. Company P&L Economics gives decision makers the information they need to manage the four variables that determine operating income:

   1. Sales revenue
   2. Value added dollars
   3. Average value added percent
   4. Total fixed costs

3. The cash from sales revenue must first pay the variable costs incurred to produce the products sold. After variable costs are paid, the remainder is value added. This value added is the cash available to pay fixed costs. After fixed costs are paid, the balance, if positive, is operating income; if negative, operating loss.

4. Company P&L Economics focuses on operating income. Operating income is what the company earns from what it does. The company produces and sells its products and services to its customers. That's what the company is organized to do.

5. The following actions increase the value added in individual product sales revenue:

   1. Reduce variable costs
   2. Increase price

3. Redesign or reformulate the product using the principles of value engineering
4. Increase sales revenue

6. Average value added percent and total value added dollars can be increased by improving the mix of products sold by selling more of the high value added products

7. Typically, sales people are asked only to manage their sales assignment to achieve a  sales revenue goal.  In that sales revenue there are variable costs. After variable costs are paid, the remainder is value added. Value added pays fixed costs, with the remainder, operating income.  Sales people can also learn Company P&L Economics, and can be asked to manage their sales assignments for both sales revenue and value added goals.

8. Company P&L Economics information helps decision makers, but more information is needed.  Also needed is information about economic conditions, the markets, the customer situations, and the competitive situation.

9. The professional salesperson asks questions beginning with the words who, how, what, why, where, and when, and listens. These questions can't be answered with a yes or no. They require a more in-depth answer, and the salesperson learns more information.

10. There are 4 ways to increase average value added percent:

1. Sell more of the high value added products.
2. Increase the value added in low value added products.
3. Increase the value added in some higher value added products.
4. Look throughout the product listing for opportunities to raise price without losing sales.
5. Develop new products with higher than average value added.

# Chapter 7

# An Operating Income Statement and Income Model that Guide Actions Needed

This chapter describes:

(1) An operating income statement constructed using Company P&L Economics measures. In this operating income statement, only the sales revenue figure is the same as in the conventional operating income statement. All the other figures are different. All the other figures are essential for effective cost and profit management.

(2) An Income Model constructed from the Company P&L Economics operating income statement. The model, constructed each reporting period, shows the current situation. Proposed actions for improvement can be entered into the model to help estimate the likely results from the action. The key measures in the model are monitored in time series charts. See Chapter 8.

## COMPANY P&L ECONOMICS OPERATING INCOME STATEMENT

Figure 9 shows a simplified operating income statement for a manufacturing company, constructed in accounting measures. This is what the managers in that company saw before they learned about Company P&L Economics.

Figure 9

Conventional Operating Income Statement, Manufacturing Company

| | | |
|---|---|---|
| Sales Revenue | | $38,724,000 |
| Cost of Goods Sold | | 35,578,000 |
| Gross Profit | | 3,146,000 |
| SGA Expenses | | 5,574,000 |
| Selling | $2,274,000 | |
| Distribution | 1,750,000 | |
| Development | 474,000 | |
| Administration | 1,076,000 | |
| Operating Income | | (2,428,000) |

This operating income statement gives us very little information. It gives us one important figure, sales revenue. It gives us a "cost of goods sold" figure which is a mixture of variable and fixed costs and tells us nothing useful for managing costs or revenue. And it tells us that the gross profit is less than the total of SGA expenses resulting in a loss for the period. In this statement there is no information to guide actions for improvement. So management is left with its own experience and judgment for the appropriate corrective action. The typical corrective action is cost reduction, applying a long-standing management idea:

Cost Reduction = Profit Improvement

Variable costs can't be cut. These costs are needed to produce the company's products. So cuts will have to be made in fixed costs. There are three categories of fixed costs—capital costs, people costs, and programmed fixed costs. Programmed fixed costs are the sales, general, and administrative costs that are not capital costs or people costs. There is not much opportunity in programmed fixed costs for significant cost reduction. Capital costs can be reduced over time by selling assets or by scrapping and recycling assets, but this may limit the company's ability to achieve its purpose. Existing capital costs are difficult to reduce. That leaves people costs as the only choice for significant, quick cost reduction.

Is cost reduction a wise decision? $10 million in cost reduction, everything else remaining the same, may result in profit improvement. But everything else does not remain the same. Everything in business is always in motion, continuously changing, with everything interrelating and affecting everything else. $10 million in cost reductions will have consequences, which may or may not include profit improvement. Some of the consequences may be harmful. Company P&L Economics offers different, more effective ways to improve profitability. The following manufacturing company experience is one example.

The operating income statement illustrated in Figure 9 was reported during the third year of continuing losses. Corporate management had ordered the traditional corrective action, "cut costs!" Losses continued. The company was a subsidiary company of a large corporation.

## THE MANUFACTURING COMPANY EXPERIENCE

The company produced calendered film and sheet and coated fabrics in a variety of formulations for many applications. The company's customers used the film and sheet in the products they made. For three years, the company had reported losses. Corporate headquarters had ordered cost reductions, and sent in cost accountants to analyze costs and recommend actions. Losses continued. The company president had heard about Company P&L Economics, and invited the corporate marketing director who knew about and had operating experience with Company P&L Economics, to work with his people to resolve the profit problem.

In a 3-hour seminar session, people from sales, accounting, purchasing, product development, manufacturing, and management learned about Company P&L Economics. They learned about variable costs and fixed costs. They learned about the operating income statement using the accounts of Company P&L Economics. They learned about the income model and ways for improving the variables that determine operating income.

After the seminar session, accounting people prepared the income statement shown in Figure 10, and compared it with their conventional operating income statement, Figure 9.

## Figure 10
## Company P&L Economics Income Statement, Manufacturing Company

| | | |
|---|---|---|
| Sales Revenue (S) | | $38,724,000 |
| Variable Costs (VC) | | 24,764,000 |
| Value Added $ (VA$) | | 13,960,000 |
| Value Added% (VA%) | | 36.05% |
| Fixed Costs (FC) | | 17,096,000 |
| People Costs | $9,018,000 | |
| Capital Costs | 5,326,000 | |
| Programmed Fixed Costs | 2,752,000 | |
| Breakeven (BE) | | 47,423,000 |
| Sales Revenue Above (Below) BE | | (8,699,000) |
| Operating Income | | (3,136,000) |

Both of these statements show the same sales revenue. All other figures are different. The conventional operating income statement has no useful information for cost or profit management. The Company P&L Economics operating income statement is filled with information that will help managers deal intelligently with whatever the situation is. This company was dealing with a loss situation. And the loss is greater in the Company P&L Economics statement because capital costs are calculated by the method shown in Figure 2, Chapter 5.

Another very important difference. The conventional operating income statement is only numbers. The Company P&L Economics operating income statement also is numbers, But these are num-bers that can also be a picture. The picture is useful as an Income Model of the company, illustrating the variables that determine the company's operating income. Figure 11 is the income model for the manufacturing company's operating income statement shown in Figure 10.

Figure 11
Income Model, Manufacturing Company ($ add 000)

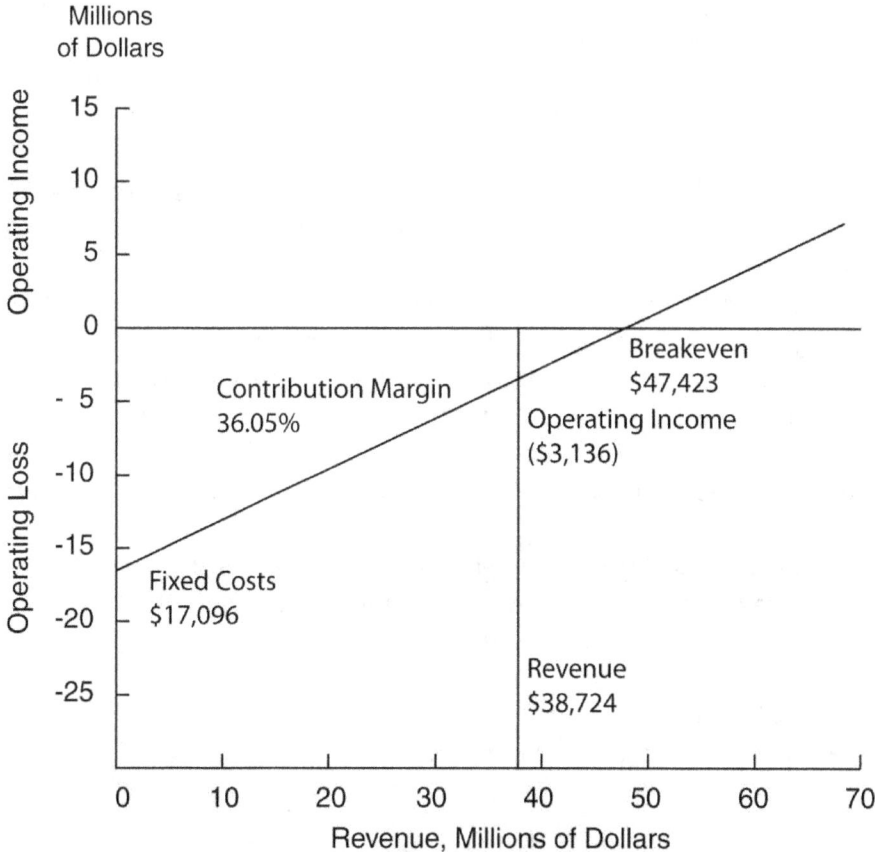

We construct models to help us understand and work with very complex subjects. We have models of the weather. We have models of the economy. Every model is a simplification of what is modeled. A model is not able to capture all the interacting variety in what is modeled. In a discussion of models, my system science and cybernetics mentor, Professor Stafford Beer, noted that models are neither good nor bad. They are more or less useful. This income model is a very useful model.

I have often used this model to illustrate the effects of changes in the variables. Using an overhead viewer and projecting the model on a screen, I place a pencil on the sales revenue line. Moving the pencil to the right shows the effect of increasing sales revenue, everything else remaining the same. Profitability improves. Moving the pencil to the left shows the effect of decreasing sales revenue. Losses increase. Place the pencil on the average value added percent line, and rotate the pencil from the line's origin on the Y axis. Rotating to the right illustrates the effects of decreases in the average value added percent. Breakeven increases. Rotating to the left illustrates the effects of increases in the average value added percent. Breakeven is reduced.

Again, with the pencil on the average value added percent line, moving the pencil vertically up shows the effect of decreasing total fixed costs. Profitability improves. Moving the pencil vertically down shows the effect of increasing total fixed costs. Losses increase. This demonstration is a good way to get into people's minds the effects and the leverages in changes in the variables that determine operating income.

At first glance, Figure 11 might look like a breakeven chart. It does show breakeven. And it shows much more. It shows the three key variables that determine operating income:

- Sales revenue
- Average value added percent
- Total fixed costs

Each of these three variables is manageable.

Models are neither good nor bad, or right or wrong; they are more or less useful.

The income model shown in Figure 11 is a very useful model, and has been used in businesses in sixteen coountries to improve profitability.

## MANUFACTURING COMPANY, ACTIONS TO BECOME PROFITABLE

Sales Revenue

Increasing sales revenue would increase value added dollars which would increase operating income. The manufacturing company shown in Figures 9, 10, and 11 had been trying to increase sales revenue, with little success. If they continued doing what they had been doing, they would continue getting what they had been getting. Losses. What could they do differently from what they had been doing that would be more effective?

Sales revenue might be increased by improving the effectiveness of the company's sales people, through clearly defined sales assignments, and training in the skills of professional salesmanship.

All salespeople Identified the major customers and prospects in their sales territories. These were about one fifth of the customers who accounted for about 80% of the territory sales revenue. These major customers were the best prospects for additional sales, too. Sales people developed sales plans for each of these major customers, and concentrated their sales efforts on these major customers. They also maintained contacts with all other customers and prospects to maintain existing business and find opportunities for additional business.

Sales territory sales reports were redesigned to list first the major customers with a total, then all others with a total, and the total of both. Sales people could see quickly the results of their major customer sales programs.

Sales training and role-playing further developed the company's sales people and other customer contact people in the skills of professional salesmanship.

These actions did strengthen the company's sales operations, and did increase sales revenue, and operating income.

Total Fixed Costs

If fixed costs could be significantly reduced, that might be a quick way to improve profitability. But the company had for three years been cutting fixed costs without improving profitability. Cutting fixed costs has many consequences. Fixed costs are reduced. But also reduced is the company's capability to do what needs to be done to create desired profitability. The company decided that further cutting of fixed costs would not be a part of their profit improvement program.

Average Value Added Percent

After the Company P&L Economics seminar, sales and accounting people began an audit of the variable costs and value added of the company's products. They assembled and analyzed variable costs, selling prices, and value added using the procedure illustrated in Figure 4 in Chapter 6. The average value added was 36% of sales revenue. But the range was extreme. Some products were close to zero percent, sales revenue barely over variable costs. Two were less than zero, with sales revenue not covering variable costs. On the high side, several products were more than 70% value added.

With the help of people in purchasing and product engineering, the sales and accounting people looked for opportunities to improve value added. Where could variable costs be reduced? Where could price be increased? Where could sales sell more of the higher value added products? What low value added, high volume products could be reformulated to a higher value added? Practical answers to these questions were found using the information developed in the product line audit, and the customer and prospect information and competitive information known by salespeople. Also helpful was the knowledge of purchasing people and product engineering people.

The search concentrated first on the higher volume products. Then product by product the search looked for other improvement opportunities. Sales people, with their knowledge of customers, markets, and the competitive situation, also looked for new market and customer opportunities. And they did find opportunities for improvement.

As a result of this work, sales, management, and others learned to be asking themselves these key questions continuously:

- How can sales revenue be increased?
- Where can we reduce variable costs?
- Where can we increase price?
- How can we sell more of our high value added products?
- Where are there improvement opportunities in redesigning or reformulating the product?
- Where are there opportunities for reducing fixed costs?

The company developed a five part action program:

1. Increase average contribution margin from 36% to 43%.

Using what they learned in their product line audit, they found ways to reduce some of their variable costs. They decided on some price increases. They found ways to sell more of the high contribution margin products. This work began in the second quarter. By year-end, average contribution margin had reached 40%, increasing value added and operating income.

2. Increase total sales revenue.

Increasing sales revenue would increase value added dollars which would increase operating income. The company had been trying to increase sales revenue, with little success. If they continued doing what they had been doing, they would continue getting what they had been getting. What could they do differently from what they had been doing that would be more effective?

Sales revenue might be increased by improving the effectiveness of the company's sales people through clearly defined sales assignments, and training in the skills of professional salesmanship. Sales assignments were reviewed, and clearly assigned.

All sales people were trained in 14 principles of professional selling:

1. Focus on and develop the sales territory, or assignment, as a business
2. Manage the sales assignment as a business to develop both revenue and value added
3. Concentrate on major customers and prospects
4. Always have an action plan for each major customer and major prospect
5. Schedule calls for efficient and effective coverage of the sales assignment
6. Maximize selling time with customers and prospects
7. Prepare each sales call, adjusting continuously during the call
8. See the right people, those who make the purchase decisions
9. "Counsel with" more than "sell to"

10. Ask questions and listen fully to the answer. To get in-depth response, begin questions with the words who, what, where, how, when, or why
11. Establish relationships
12. Develop proposals that are good for the customer or prospect, and good also for the company
13. Get the order
14. Follow up and assure customer satisfaction

All salespeople Identified the major customers and prospects in their sales territories. These were about one fifth of the customers who accounted for about 80% of the territory sales revenue. These largest customers were the best prospects for additional sales, too. Sales people developed sales plans for each of these major customers, and concentrated their sales efforts on these major customers. They also maintained contacts with all other customers and prospects to maintain existing business and find opportunities for additional business.

The company's major customers could also become the company's largest sales losses if some of this business is lost. So sales people maintained close contact, and continuously built strong relationships with each major customer. In addition to selling, sales people worked to prevent losses. They also worked to develop additional business. Major customers also can be a good opportunity for additional, new business. Sales people were trained in Company P&L Economics and were involved in the business management of their sales assignments. They had both sales revenue and value added objectives. Both were included in the incentive compensation plan.

Sales training and role-playing further developed the company's sales people and other customer contact people in the skills of professional salesmanship.

These actions did strengthen the company's sales operations, and increased sales revenue, and operating income.

3. Set value added objectives for new products.

Product development was constantly working on new product projects for specific customers. With the need to increase average value added percent, sales and product development agreed to set a value added goal of 50% or more for new products.

Of course the aim is for value added dollars. So if a new product project could not be developed for 50% or more value added, 45% or 40% at the projected sales volume might produce very satisfactory value added dollars. People using Company P&L Economics consider all the variables all the time.

In this company there were always new products in development, with short development times. Adding a value added objective did improve new product value added percent. New products became an important part of major customer sales plans. Within a few months, new product sales began to increase sales revenue, and to improve, also, average value added percent.

4. Improve productivity in manufacturing operations.

To support increased sales volume without increasing fixed costs the company would need to increase production output with no major new capital investment. The company had been investigating lean manufacturing technology, and began applying some of this technology in their operations. Programs were developed for:

- Reducing setup time
- Reducing scrap and rework
- Automating in-process testing and quality control
- Increasing throughput rates
- Within two years capacity increased more than 50% with no major capital investment.

5. Monitor and control fixed costs.

Cutting fixed costs was not a part of the profit improvement program. But controlling fixed costs was. The company monitored total fixed costs monthly and prepared a 3-month moving average of total fixed costs to detect any trends developing. They also monitored monthly the three components of total fixed costs: people costs, capital costs, and programmed fixed costs.

Implementing this 5-part program, by year-end the company was profitable. In the following year the company achieved its profitability objectives. Average value added increased from 36% to 43%. The major customer sales program increased sales revenue more than ten percent, with growth continuing. Increased sales plus increased value added increased operating income to $2 million. The same people, working hard, had produced three years of losses. Now, working hard but differently, they were producing and growing profitability. Morale brightened, from gloominess to happiness. This happy result began with learning and applying Company P&L Economics.

Service company income model

An income model for a service company with few or no variable costs will look very different. A service firm, such as a law firm, a consulting firm, or an accounting firm will have few, or no, variable costs in their work processes. All of their costs are fixed costs. Every dollar of revenue contributes a dollar to the payment of fixed costs. Breakeven is reached when revenue equals total fixed costs. The income model for a service company with no variable costs will look like Figure 12.

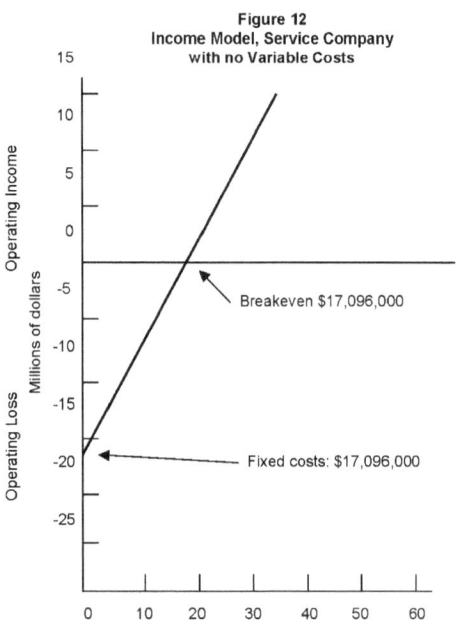

Figure 12
Income Model, Service Company
with no Variable Costs

## WILL ACCOUNTANTS LIKE COMPANY P&L ECONOMICS?

I have worked with business people in more than a hundred businesses, in sixteen countries, applying Company P&L Economics in their businesses. Our work began with learning sessions. In a morning session we could discuss Company P&L Economics principles, the methods and measures derived from these principles, and the operating income statement and income model using these new measures. We discussed also examples from the experience of other companies. We discussed what's in this book. We were then ready to begin applying these new concepts, methods, and measures.

To apply the concepts and methods, we needed the measures. This would be a job for the accountants. All the data needed is in the company's chart of accounts and product cost records which the accountants work with daily, and know thoroughly. What would be their reaction to this something-more-to-do? They already felt overworked, and pressured by due dates. I wondered if they would resist this additional work. They did not. Accountants typically enjoyed developing the Company P&L Economics measures, for two reasons:

1.  The work was easy to do; much simpler and much easier than their accounting reports. And some of the Company P&L Economics totals do not need to be precisely right, they need only to be usefully right.

2.  They saw that these new measures would help their company improve its operating income and profitability. They were participating in making this improvement happen.

## IMPORTANT IDEAS IN CHAPTER 7
## AN OPERATING INCOME STATEMENT AND INCOME MODEL THAT GUIDE ACTIONS NEEDED

1.  The conventional operating income statement has no useful information for cost or profit management. If the statement shows that the company made its numbers, all's fine. If profitability is low,

there is no information on what can be done to increase profitability. The most usual action is: cut costs.

2. The Company P&L Economics operating income statement is filled with information that will help managers deal intelligently with whatever the situation is.

3. For companies using Company P&L Economics, in a low profit or loss situation, the first response is finding ways to increase value added.

4. Every model is a simplification, and cannot capture all the interacting variety in what is modeled. Models are neither good nor bad. They are more or less useful. The Company P&L Economics income model is a very useful model.

5. The Company P&L Economics income model illustrates the relationships of the three key variables that determine operating income:

   - Sales revenue
   - Average value added percent
   - Total fixed costs
   - Each of these three variables is manageable.

6. Sales people trained in Company P&L Economics will have both sales revenue and value added objectives. Both can be included in the incentive compensation plan.

7. Accountants typically enjoy developing the Company P&L Economics measures, for two reasons:

   1. The work is easy to do; much simpler than their accounting reports.
   2. They see how these new measures help their company control costs and improve profitability. They are participating in making this improvement happen.

# Chapter 8

# Managing Operating Income

Company P&L Economics gives management, and decision-makers throughout the organization, the information they need to manage the variables that determine the company's operating income. Operating income is what the company earns from what it does. Desired company profitability begins with achieving the needed operating income. Company P&L Economics enables decision-makers to manage all the variables that determine operating income. These are the variables; all can be measured, all can be managed:

1. Sales revenue
2. Variable costs
3. Value added
4. Average value added percent
5. Total fixed costs and its three components:
   Total people costs
   Total capital costs
   Total programmed fixed costs

All five of these variables can be measured and managed to maintain and improve operating Income.

- Decision makers using Company P&L Economics have the information they need to manage all five of these variables to help them achieve desired operating income.
- Managers have the information on sales revenue that helps them improve sales revenue; and helps them also improve the profitability of sales revenue.
- Sales, accounting, product development, and purchasing people have the information they need to manage variable costs and improve value added.
- Decision makers have the information they need to control total fixed costs in relation to the value added cash earned.

All five of these variables can be managed to create desired operating income.

In almost all companies and business units today, decision makers have only the figure for sales revenue and a figure for operating income to work with. They do not have information on the variables, and do not understand the variables listed above. Using Company P&L Economics, they can measure and manage:

1. Sales revenue
2. Variable costs
3. Value added
4. Average value added percent
5. Total fixed costs and its three components:
   a. Total people costs
   b. Total capital costs
   c. Total programmed fixed costs

What these measures are, and how they interact create:

6. Operating income

$$Sales\ Revenue - Variable\ Costs = Value\ Added$$

$$Value\ Added - Total\ Fixed\ Costs = Operating\ Income$$

When there is a profit problem, changes in some combination of these variables will usually be a solution. Typically, creating value is the most effective solution to a profit problem. Creating value will focus on items 1, 2, 3, and 4 in the above listing. In addition to creating value, controlling or reducing some fixed costs may be a part of the solution.

## A FIVE-PART PROCESS

Company P&L Economics helps managers and decision makers at all levels improve sales revenue, control costs, create value added, and achieve desired operating income.

1. A company or business unit is structured to create value for customers. Company P&L Economics measures and monitors the value created in time series charts.

2. The measure of value created for customers is value added dollars. Company P&L Economics measures value added dollars and average value added percent, and monitors these measures in time series charts. By increasing value added in present sales revenue, decision makers can increase the profitability of sales revenue.

3. The structure of the company or business unit is the combination of its resources, which are represented by its total fixed costs:
   People Costs +
   Capital Costs +
   Programmed Fixed Costs = Total Fixed Costs
   Company P&L Economics measures and monitors total fixed costs, and each of its three components, in time series charts.

4. The structure of the company creates value for customers:

   In the 1860s, Studebaker built the rugged conestoga wagons that carried settlers into the West.
   In 1906, Henry Ford invented the assembly line and built a car that anyone could buy; one-third the cost of other cars.
   In 1998, Google made the world's information easily accessible and useful
   In 2004, Face Book offered a new kind of social networking for Harvard Students.
   In 2011, low and zero emissions cars appeared.

5. The task for managers and decision makers is to earn enough value added dollars to pay all structure costs—all fixed costs—and enough more for a desired operating income. Company P&L Economics provides the information needed for this task.

This 5-part process successfully done provides good jobs for employees, Incentives for high achievement, returns for share-holders, and a credit rating that supports innovation and growth. Company P&L Economics guides decision makers through this 5-part process.

## GOALS AND MEASURES

To manage operating income, The following are essential goals and measures for managing the variables to achieve desired operating income.

| What to Measure: | Measure | To Help Understand |
|---|---|---|
| Total sales revenue | 12-month moving total, centered | Trend and changes |
| Monthly variance from year ago | 3-month moving average, centered | Current changes |
| Each major segment of total sales revenue | 12-month moving total, centered | Trend and changes |
| Monthly variance from year ago | 3-month moving average, centered | Current changes |

Sales revenue goals will typically be set for 2 years ahead and for 5 years ahead. Some companies might wish to set a longer term goal, 10 years, or 25 years. 2 and 5 year goals can be plotted on the 12-month moving total chart. The management task is to get from the present 12-month total, to the 2-year goal. At the time the budget goals are set, it's helpful to draw a straight line from the data point for the present 12-month total to the 2-year goal.

As new 12-month totals are plotted each month, the 12-month moving total will track performance toward the goals. The line drawn to the goal will help in assessing whether or not sales revenue is on track toward the goal. At each monthly closing the question is not, "Did we make the numbers?" There are no monthly numbers. Instead there is the measure of progress toward the goal. At each monthly closing the question is, "Are we on track toward our goal?" The answer to this question leads to whatever actions are appropriate.

The time series charts plus the sales people's knowledge of market conditions provide reliable answers to the question, "Are we on track toward our goal?" With each month's closing, Company P&L Economics data and the knowledge of sales people and other company people on market conditions, provides information for any corrective actions needed.

Sales revenue is manageable. As discussed in Chapter 6, there are ways to increase sales revenue, and ways to increase the profitability of sales revenue. At each monthly closing the data can be reported. But most useful will be the charted data, as illustrated in Figure 13.

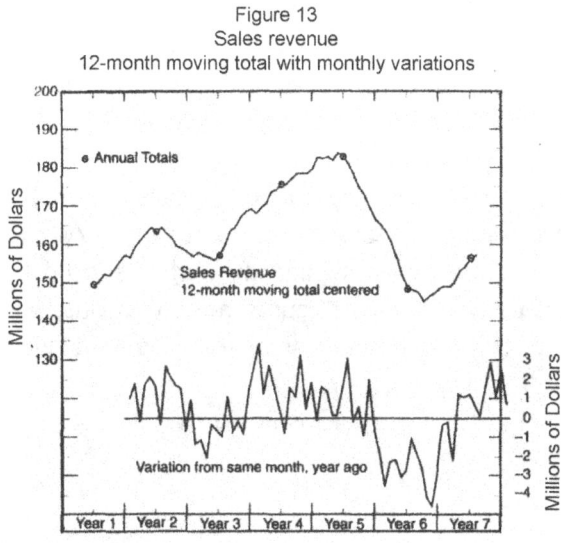

Figure 13
Sales revenue
12-month moving total with monthly variations

Figure 13 shows the sales revenue 12-month moving total over a seven year period. At each monthly closing, the new 12-month total was added to the plot. Fiscal year totals are plotted at the midpoints of the 12 month total. For this company, the fiscal year was the calendar year, so fiscal year totals are plotted at June 30, the mid-point of the fiscal year. Fiscal year totals are shown by the bullets on the chart at June 30, the mid-points of the fiscal years. At each monthly closing, the variation from the same month a year ago was plotted on the curve at the bottom of the chart. To smooth variations in the curve a 3-month moving average could be used for this chart.

These two charts, plus the knowledge company sales people have of customers, market conditions, and the competitive situation help company people understand the current situation and outlook. In this company, at the end of year 2, 12-month sales revenue was $163,570,000. This number is plotted on the chart at the midpoint of year 2, June 30.

Management at that time was developing a budget for year 3, and with sales rising anticipated that a significant increase in sales revenue should be budgeted for year 3. Sales and marketing, however, was sensitive to current customer, market, and competitive conditions. They thought the downturn in monthly variations from a year ago was signaling a likely down turn in sales revenue. They urged no increase in the budget for sales revenue in year 3. Sales revenue in year 3 declined to $155,235,000.

Sales revenue grew strongly through years 4 and 5. Then there followed a sharp decline in sales revenue in year 6. At the end of year six, with sales revenue down significantly, what should be the budget for year 7? Sales people, aware of customer situations, were optimistic. The chart of monthly variations was heading up. And sales revenue did increase in year 7.

The data format for Figure 13 is illustrated in Figure 14.

**Figure 14**
**Data for Fig. 13**
**12-Month moving totals, plotted at mid-point, with**
**Monthly variance from year-ago**

| | Sales Revenue | Monthly Varience | 12-Month Moving Total, Centered |
|---|---|---|---|
| Year 1 | | | |
| Jan | 10,992 | | |
| Feb | 11,748 | | |
| Mar | 14,765 | | |
| | | | |
| Apr | 12,595 | | |
| May | 13,103 | | |
| Jun | 12,707 | | 149,780* |
| | | | |
| Jul | 12,304 | | 150,656 |
| Aug | 10,446 | | 152,410 |
| Sep | 12,238 | | 152,103 |
| | | | |
| Oct | 13,836 | | |
| Nov | 12,602 | | 155,761 |
| Dec | 12,444 | | 157,310 |
| | | | |
| Year 2 | | | |
| Jan | 11,868 | 876 | 156,808 |
| Feb | 13,502 | 1,754 | 159,410 |
| Mar | 14,458 | (307) | 161,376 |
| | | | |
| Apr | 14,252 | 1,657 | 162,960 |
| May | 15,104 | 2,001 | 164,381 |
| Jun | 14,256 | 1,549 | 163,570* |
| | | | |
| Jul | 11,802 | (502) | 164,415 |
| Aug | 13,048 | 2,602 | 162,970 |
| Sep | 14,204 | 1,966 | 161,667 |
| | | | |
| Oct | 14,186 | 1,584 | 159,460 |
| Nov | 15,257 | 1,421 | 158,928 |
| Dec | 11,633 | (811) | 158,117 |

* 12 Month moving totals, plotted at mid point

## Sales revenue goals

Companies using Company P&L Economics will set goals for sales revenue for a longer term than the fiscal year. Goals will typically be set for 2 years and 5 years, and even longer. Goals are not constrained to fiscal year periods. They are set for whatever time frame is appropriate; longer than the fiscal year, or shorter. Companies using the continuous budgeting idea set budget goals for whatever time period is appropriate, from months, to a few years. [4]

For sales revenue, goals for 2 and 5 years ahead are usually practical. Control is not to a monthly budget. Control is progress toward the achievement of the 2 year goal. That may sound like a fuzzy control. But with the control of a 12-month moving total, like Figure 13, the control is actionable with each month's closing. The data and the chart will show whether or not the company is on track toward the goal.

This is a new and different method of setting the budget goal, measuring performance, and continuously taking appropriate actions. This different method is much more effective in achieving desired results than the conventional fiscal year budget process.

Value added goals

Value added goals are the most important goals for the company. Value added is what the company creates using its human and capital resources. Value added creates operating income:

$$\text{Value Added} - \text{Total Fixed Costs} = \text{Operating Income}$$

Operating income creates company profit. The company is structured and operated to create value for customers. Value added is the measure of that value. Total fixed costs are the company's costs for the company structure. Total variable costs are the company's costs for producing and delivering company products and services to customers. After sales revenue pays the total variable costs in those sales, the remaining sales revenue cash is the company's value added. These value added dollars pay fixed costs, with the balance operating income.

The key measure for goal setting is average value added percent. Goals for average value added percent will typically be set for less than a year, with also a longer term goal. First, management will evaluate the present situation and recent history, as described in the time series charts. They might then set a short term goal for some improvement for a few months ahead, with a longer term goal for greater improvement some twelve or fifteen months ahead. If the current average value added percent is 40%, management might set a goal of 42% in six months, and 45% in ten or twelve months. [4]

An improvement goal like this could only be set if the company has an action plan for increasing value added product by product, and transaction by transaction. As described in this book, options include:

1. Reducing variable costs for some products
2. Selling more of the high value added products

**3.** Redesigning or reformulating some products, using the principles of value engineering
**4.** Substituting products with higher value added
**5.** Developing new products with higher value added
**6.** Raising some prices

Total Fixed Cost Goals

To set a goal for total fixed costs, the first task is to determine what the company's fixed costs are. These costs are known by their individual accounts, but the totals are not known. The three classifications of fixed costs are: people costs, capital costs, and programmed fixed costs. To measure total fixed costs, classify the many individual fixed cost line item accounts into these three categories:

**1.** People costs. All employment and benefit costs, and other costs incurred for company employees
**2.** Capital costs, all the capital costs illustrated in Figure 2
**3.** Programmed fixed costs, all sales, general, and administrative costs that are not people costs or capital costs

All fixed costs can be classified into these three categories.

Assemble monthly data for the last 2 years, and for the current year-to-date for:

**1.** Total people costs
**2.** Total capital costs
**3.** Total programmed fixed costs
**4.** Total fixed costs

For each of the above, plot the data on a time series chart. Or, usually better, plot a 3-month moving average to smooth the curve. Plot each 3-month average at the middle month. Figure 3 illustrates this kind of a chart. These charts, updated at each monthly closing, will help management control total fixed costs in relation to the value added dollars and desired operating income.

Set a goal for total fixed costs for 6 months ahead, and for 12 or 18 months ahead. Put the goal on the time series chart, and evaluate progress at each monthly closing and update of the chart. Take actions as needed.

Similarly, set goals for each of the three components of total fixed costs—people costs, capital costs, and programmed fixed costs—for a short term ahead and for a longer term ahead. Put these goals on time series charts. With each monthly closing, update the charts, and take actions as appropriate.

Operating income goals

Operating income is what the company earns from what it does. Sales revenue minus variable costs equals value added. Value added minus total fixed costs equals operating income. Managers and decision makers watch the time series tracking of operating income, and the variables that determine operating income. The key measures:

1. Operating income, 12-month moving total plotted at the midpoint of each 12-    month period

If the company is aiming for increased operating income, there will typically be a short-term goal, and a longer term goal.  Decision makers, seeing the12-month moving total and variances from year-ago, are aware of current trends and changes.  They are also aware of current business conditions, customer situations, and the competitive environment. They also know about:

(1). The Company P&L Economics methods for improving the profitability of existing sales revenue

(2). The Company P&L Economics guides for increasing sales revenue

With this information they can set a short-term goal for operating income, perhaps, 5 months, and a 10 or 12-month goal for greater improvement.

2. 3-month moving average of the monthly variation in operating income from a year ago. This chart signals any changes developing.

## OPERATING INCOME STATEMENT

The top line in the income statement reports total sales revenue. That is the figure that management attempts to manage to bring cash into the company. But total sales revenue is not the measure of cash brought into the company. Before any cash is available from total sales revenue, all the variable costs incurred for that sales revenue (materials, parts, components, etc.) must be paid. After these costs are paid the balance is value added. Value added is the cash brought into the company in its total sales revenue.

In a business with few or no variable costs, such as a consulting firm, a law firm, or an accounting firm, there may be few or no variable costs. All, or almost all, of sales revenue is value added.

Value added is the company's most important performance measure. It is the measure of the value the company creates for its customers. This value created for customers first pays for all the structural costs of the company:

Total People Costs +
Total Capital Costs +
Total Programed Fixed Costs =Total Fixed costs

The balance after paying total fixed costs, if positive, is operating income; if negative; operating loss.

Company P&L Economics reports at each monthly closing:

- Total sales revenue
- Total variable costs
- Value added dollars
- Average value added percent
- Sales revenue for each major segment of total sales revenue
- Value added for each major segment of total sales revenue
- Average value added percent for each major segment of total sales revenue
- Total people costs
- Total capital costs
- Total programmed fixed costs
- Total fixed costs
- Breakeven
- Sales revenue above (or below) breakeven
- Operating income

These data (except for the data on major segments of sales revenue) is reported monthly in the operating income statement described in Figure 10 in Chapter 7, and repeated here for reference:

Figure 10 (Repeated)
Company P&L Economics Income Statement, Manufacturing Company

| | |
|---|---:|
| Sales Revenue (S) | $38,724,000 |
| Variable Costs (VC) | 24,764,000 |
| Value Added $ (VA$) | 13,960,000 |
| Value Added% (VA%) | 36.05% |
| Fixed Costs (FC) | 17,096,000 |
|   People Costs | $9,018,000 |
|   Capital Costs | 5,326,000 |
|   Programmed Fixed Costs | 2,752,000 |
| Breakeven (BE) | 47,423,000 |
| Sales Revenue Above (Below) BE | (8,699,000) |
| Operating Income | (3,136,000) |

Using Company P&L Economics, managers and decision-makers at all levels see this data with each month's closing. But seeing this current data is not enough. They need to be aware also of how these data are changing. And this is accomplished by monitoring time series data of the key measures:

| Key measures | Time Series | Showing |
|---|---|---|
| Sales revenue | 12-month moving total, centered | Trend and changes |
| Sales revenue, variation from year ago | 3-month moving average, centered | Current change happening |
| Value added dollars | 12-month moving total, centered | Trend and changes |
| Value added dollars, variation from year ago | 3-month moving average, centered | Current change happening |
| Value added percent | 3-month moving average, centered | Current change happening |
| Breakeven | 3-month moving average | Current change happening |
| Total fixed costs | 3-month moving average | Current change happening |

| | | |
|---|---|---|
| People costs | 3-month moving average | Current change happening |
| Capital costs | 3-month moving average | Current change happening |
| Programmed fixed costs | 3-month moving average | Current change happening |
| Operating Income | 12-month moving total, centered | Trend and changes |

Figure 3 from Chapter 5 is repeated here to illustrate the usefulness of the monthly time series of total fixed costs. Figure 3 shows the 3-month moving average of total fixed costs over a six year period, for the manufacturing company whose sales revenue is charted in Figure 13, Figure 3 was the first time managers in this manufacturing company had ever seen a total of their fixed costs. This chart was first prepared during year 6, when the company had a profit problem.

**Figure 3**
**Total fixed costs, manufacturing company**
**3-month moving average**

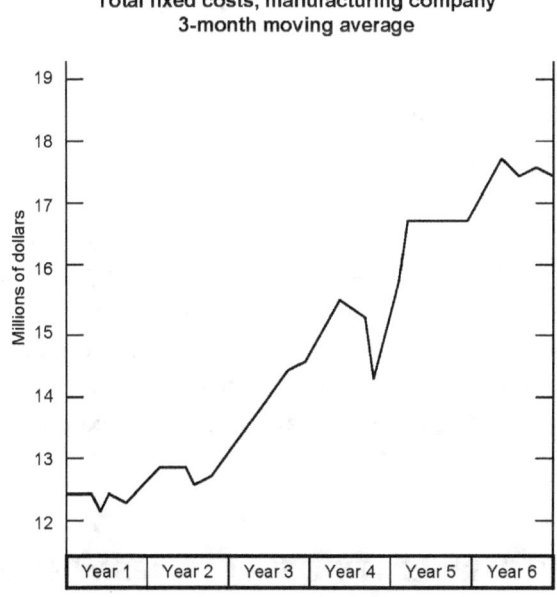

Management, now knowing their total fixed costs, were able to prevent any further increase in years 6 and 7; even reducing total fixed costs slightly during year 6. At the same time, sales and marketing were able to increase total sales revenue in year 7, and this increase continued in year 8. See Figure 13.

All of the above measures are monitored monthly to inform management and other company people on changing conditions. But we only need to budget 5 key measures:

1. Total sales revenue*
2. Value added dollars
3. Average value added percent
4. Total fixed costs
5. Operating income

*For additional information on total sales revenue, it is useful to budget, measure, and monitor each major component of total sales revenue, including for each major component:

- Sales revenue, 12-month moving total, centered
- Sales revenue, 3-month moving average of variation from year ago, centered
- Value added dollars, 12-month moving total, centered
- Average value added percent, 3-month moving average, centered

All of these data are essential for effectively managing operating income. All of these data are available in Company P&L Economics. None of these data are available to decision makers in the measures they are now using. Accounting is best used for what it is designed for—financial and tax reporting. Company P&L Economics is best used for what it is designed for— managing revenue, fixed costs, and operating income.

## COMPLEXITY DETERMINES WHERE DECISIONS ARE MADE

A company is a viable, purposeful, very complex, probabilistic system:

- Viable: Capable of living successfully in its environments

- Purposeful: Exists for a purpose
- Very complex: Complex beyond the comprehension of any individual or group of individuals
- Probabilistic: All internal and external actions and relationships perform more-or-less but not exactly as planned or expected
- System: a group of functions and entities that together continuously does what it is organized to do.

Every company is structured to achieve its purpose. The company itself is very, very complex. And the company lives in and works in the environments outside the company: the commercial environment, economic environment, technical environment, social environment, political environment, educational environment, and the ecological environment. Each of these environments is also very, very complex.

The very, very complex company, lives and works in very, very complex environments. Both the company and its environments continue to grow in complexity at an accelerating rate. The complexity in the company's operations is huge, and accelerating. The complexity in the company's environments is much greater, and the growth in this environmental complexity is also accelerating. Complexity determines where and how Company P&L Economics concepts, methods, and measures are used.

A large corporation might have several, or many operating units. Company P&L Economics is useful at the corporate level only for the management of corporate fixed costs. The corporate level does not produce and sell products and services.

Company P&L Economics is used in the operating units for cost and profit management. Operating units do make and sell products and services. They have variable costs to manage. They earn a value added that needs to be managed. They have fixed costs to manage. They have operating income to manage. Company P&L Economics helps managers and decision makers in the operating units manage all of these to achieve desired operating income.

The corporate level wants good results from its operating units. But the corporate level has to rely on the people in each operating unit for these results. An operating unit is a very, very complex operation, with its complexity steadily and rapidly increasing. The environments an operating unit lives in and works in are even more complex, with their complexity increasingly accelerating. All this complexity in operations and their environments can be dealt with successfully only by the people in the operating units.

The huge complexity in an operating unit and its environments can only be managed by the huge capability in the people managing and working in the operating unit. People at the corporate level have the capability to manage corporate affairs and to structure the operating units. They lack the capability needed to manage affairs in an operating unit. That capability exists only within the operating unit. Any corporate intervention in the operations of an operating unit will more harm than help.

## AN EXAMPLE

A large European company, part of an American multi-national corporation, at midyear was reporting a projected loss for the year of $5 million. Over recent years, the company had expanded its markets, and its products and services, planning further growth. But business conditions had worsened in its market areas. The managing director was anticipating recovery in the following year. The president of the American corporation, pressed for earnings, decided to take tough action. He replaced the company's managing director with a finance manager from corporate headquarters. He instructed the finance manager to take control and cut costs.

The new managing director immediately cut costs. He laid off employees, including several management and technical people. Several top management people left the company. One technical group left the company and formed a new company that competed in the same markets. The new managing director sold the company's headquarters building and moved into leased space. He sold the company's art collection. At the end of the year the company lost $20 million. Back in the U.S. the corporate President commented, "Think how bad it would have been if I hadn't taken tough action." The company continued on for a few more years, moderately profitable, and was then sold.

If the president hadn't taken tough action, the loss would have been something like $5 million. The following year market conditions improved. The company would have been ready for growth. Sales revenue would have increased, and the company would have earned the desired profitability. But the corporate intervention and cost reduction had destroyed the company.

A corporate level intervention in an operating unit's operations will always more hurt than help.

## IMPORTANT IDEAS IN CHAPTER 8
## MANAGING OPERATING INCOME

1.  Company P&L Economics enables decision-makers to manage all the variables to achieve desired operating income:

    1.  Sales revenue
    2.  Variable costs
    3.  Value added
    4.  Average value added percent
    5.  Total fixed costs and its three components:
        Total people costs
        Total capital costs
        Total programmed fixed costs
    All five can be managed to maintain and improve operating Income

2.  A company or business unit is structured to create value for customers. Company P&L Economics measures the fixed costs of the structure, and the value created for customers.

3.  Short and long term goals and performance measures can be set for the key measures that determine operating income:

    (1) Sales Revenue: 12-month moving total, and monthly variance from year ago
    (2) Value added dollars: 12-month moving total
    (3) Average value added percent: 3-month moving average
    (4) Total fixed costs: 3-month moving average

4.  Value added is the company's most important performance measure. It is the measure of the value the company created for its customers. It is the measure that creates operating income:

Value Added – Total Fixed Costs = Operating Income.

5. Seeing current data is not enough. Managers and decision makers need to be aware also of how these data are changing. And this is accomplished by monitoring time series charts of the key measures.

6. Accounting is best used for what it was designed for—financial and tax reporting. Company P&L Economics is best used for what it was designed for—managing revenue, costs, and operating income.

7. The huge complexity in an operating unit and its environments can only be managed by the people in the operating unit. People at the corporate level manage corporate affairs and structure the operating units. Corporate people lack the knowledge resources needed to manage affairs within an operating unit. Corporate intervention in operations management will more harm than help.

# Chapter 9

# Economic Productivity

The first line in the income statement, Sales Revenue, is the first measure of success for the company, or P & L business unit. In successful companies, managing the top line becomes an important part of managing the bottom line. Sales revenue pays variable costs and provides the value added dollars that pays fixed costs and provides operating income. There is always opportunity for change and improvement.

This Chapter presents a measure of the company's effectiveness in creating value added. The value added created by the company is the most important figure needed for cost and profit management. Yet few companies today calculate and manage this measure. Company P&L Economics does calculate this measure and provides decision-makers the information they need to manage this measure. The formula for value added, is simple:

$$\text{Sales Revenue} - \text{Variable Costs} = \text{Value Added}$$

Value added is the measure of the value the company creates for its customers. Economic productivity measures show how effectively and how efficiently the company uses its people resources, its capital resources, and its other fixed costs to create value for customers. Monitoring the company's economic productivity will indicate any developing changes in operating income months before such changes show up in financial reporting.

## ECONOMIC PRODUCTIVITY MEASURES

Measures of economic productivity will help managers understand past and present profit performance. But the measure is most useful for determining actions needed to achieve desired operating income. The formula for Economic Productivity:

$$P\$ = \frac{VA}{L + K + PFC}$$

P$ — Economic Productivity
VA—Value Added
L — People Costs
K — Capital Costs
PFC — Programmed Fixed Costs (all SG&A costs that are not people costs or capital costs)

In calculating the formula for economic productivity:

1.  Value Added (VA) is sales revenue minus variable costs. Value Added is calculated as total sales revenue minus the variable costs incurred to produce the products sold. Variable costs include all materials, parts, components, subassemblies, coatings, adhesives, fasteners and whatever else was purchased from outside suppliers and used in the production of the products sold. In a service business, such as an accounting firm or a law firm, there may be few, if any, variable costs. In service businesses, value added may be the same as, or close to, sales revenue.

2. Labor cost (L) is the total cost of all company people, including wages, salaries, incentive compensation, benefits, payroll taxes, and any other costs incurred for company people. All company people are involved in creating value added.

3. Capital cost (K) is the cost of the capital inputs used to produce the value added. Company P&L Economics adjusts for inflation when calculating depreciation. Depreciating the inflation-adjusted values assures the availability of the cash needed to replace the assets. For information on measures of capital costs, see Figure 2 in Chapter 5.

4. Programmed fixed costs (PFC) are the sales, general, and administrative costs that are not people costs or capital costs.

## Partial Measures

The partial measures of economic productivity can also be measured, using the following formulas:

Economic productivity of labor:   $P\$(L) = \dfrac{VA}{L}$

Economic productivity of capital:   $P\$(K) = \dfrac{VA}{K}$

Economic productivity of programmed fixed costs:   $P\$(PFC) = \dfrac{VA}{PFC}$

### Economic Productivity Data, Company A

Figure 15 shows the economic productivity data for Company A, a manufacturing division of a large corporation.

**Figure 15**
Company A, 5-Year Economic Productivity Data

|  | Year 1 | | Year 3 | | Year 5 | |
|---|---|---|---|---|---|---|
|  | $ | index | $ | index | $ | index |
| 1. Sales Revenue | 173,614 | 100 | 201,184 | 116 | 219,874 | 127 |
| 2. Variable Costs | 88,616 | 100 | 106,668 | 120 | 118,620 | 134 |
| 3. Value Added (VA) | 84,853 | 100 | 94,516 | 111 | 101,254 | 119 |
| 4. People Costs (L) | 18,714 | 100 | 23,736 | 127 | 32,514 | 174 |
| 5. Capital Costs(K) | 32,243 | 100 | 39,663 | 123 | 54,741 | 170 |
| 6. Programmed Fixed Costs (PFC) | 9,550 | 100 | 11,308 | 118 | 14,380 | 151 |
| 7. L+K+PFC | 60,507 | 100 | 74,707 | 123 | 101,635 | 168 |
| 8. Economic Productivity* | 140 | | 127 | | 100 | |
| 9. Economic Profit | 24,346 | | 19,809 | | (381) | |

*Line 3 ÷ Line 7

This simple statement begins with sales revenue and variable costs, to calculate value added. Value added is the measure of the value added by the company in producing the products and services the company sold to its customers. Value added is total sales revenue minus the variable costs (purchased materials, parts, components used to produce the products sold).

## EVALUATING THE DATA

Economic productivity data are essential for managing costs and profitability. Of these data, only the figure for sales revenue is known by decision-makers today. None of the other numbers are known by management people involved in cost and profit management. Company people do have a figure for operating income. However, the figure used here for operating income is lower than the accounting figure because Company P&L Economics increases capital costs. Using the data in the company's chart of accounts, and product cost data, all these figures can be easily calculated. All are calculated and continuously monitored in Company P&L Economics.

Variable Costs. These are the costs of the purchased materials, parts, components, and energy used to produce the products sold. These costs are available in product cost records. Current costs would be the best costs to use, but LIFO costs may be more readily available, and are usually satisfactory.

Value Added. Value added is total sales revenue minus the variable costs incurred to produce the products sold (purchased materials, parts, assemblies, components, fasteners, coatings, etc. used in producing the products sold). Value added is the value created by the company.

The company is a structure of people, capital, and programmed fixed costs. The job of this structure is to produce value added. Value added dollars pay for this structure. Value added dollars in excess of the cost of the company's structure is operating income. Managers today are not aware of this relationship. They don't know their company's value added. They don't know their company's total fixed costs, and the totals of the three components of total fixed costs:

1. Total people costs
2. Total capital costs
3. Total programmed fixed costs

Using Company P&L Economics, managers and decision-makers see these data with every monthly closing, and monitor trends and changes in trends in monthly updated time series charts.

Total Fixed Costs. Total fixed costs is the total of the three categories of fixed costs: people costs, capital costs, and programmed fixed costs. Managers today don't know these totals. They know these costs only in hundreds of individual line-item accounts. Each of the accounts has a name. But none are identified as fixed costs, or identified as people costs, capital costs, or programmed fixed costs. There may be hundreds or thousands of individual line item accounts in people costs. There may be hundreds or thousands of line item accounts in capital costs. There may be hundreds or thousands of line item accounts in programmed fixed costs. Managers manage all of these accounts, one at a time. Managing all of the accounts one at a time does not manage the total of all of them. Today's management of fixed costs leaves total fixed costs uncontrolled.

But total fixed costs can be measured and controlled using the monthly measures of Company P&L Economics. Each monthly close reports:

- Total fixed costs, 3-month moving average chart, centered
- Total people costs, 3-month moving average chart, centered
- Total capital costs, 3-month moving average chart, centered
- Total programmed fixed costs, 3-month moving average chart, centered

Each monthly closing adds one month to these charts.

In addition, Company P&L Economics reports monthly:

- Total sales revenue
- Total variable costs
- Value added dollars
- Average value added percent
- Breakeven
- Sales revenue above (or below) breakeven
- Operating income (including the higher capital costs as explained in Figure 2)
- Updated time series charts for each of the above

These data, plus the knowledge company people have of customer, market, and economic and competitive conditions, enable wise decisions on actions needed. Always the focus is on what needs to be done to move the company toward its revenue and profit goals.

Economic Productivity monitors each of the six key measures each month, tracking trends and changes. Accounting reports sales revenue. That's where economic productivity gets the number. Company P&L Economics calculates the variable costs in sales revenue each month. Sales revenue minus variable costs equals value added. That's how economic productivity gets the figure for value added.

Accounting also reports operating income. But here the accounting number and the economic productivity number will differ. The economic measure of capital costs uses the method shown in Figure 2 to calculate capital costs. This results in higher, and more realistic, capital costs than shown in the accounting record, and correspondingly lower operating income.

All of the numbers used in Company P&L Economics can be calculated from the company's chart of accounts, but they are not calculated and reported in the accounting record:

1. Value added
2. People costs
3. Capital costs
4. Programmed fixed costs
5. Total fixed costs
6. Operating income (including capital costs higher than reported by accounting)

These six figures are essential for managing costs and operating income.

Value added is the dollar measure of the value the company creates. The company uses the company's total fixed costs to produce this value added. There are three components of total fixed costs: (1) the company's people, (2) the company's capital resources, and (3) the company's programmed fixed costs. Company people use the company's capital equipment and the company's programmed fixed costs to produce value added.

Company A is a manufacturing division of a major corporation. Company A had struggled with a profit problem as it was developing its budget for the next fiscal year. To help understand their situation and how to fix it, they examined the company's Economic Productivity trends over the previous five years. The results are shown in Figure 15, and the trends summarized in Figure 16.

**Figure 16**
**Company A, Economic Productivity Summary**
**5 years actual, and budget for year 6**

| | Year 1 | | Year 3 | | Year 5 | | Year 6 Budget | |
|---|---|---|---|---|---|---|---|---|
| | Measure | Index | Measure | Index | Measure | Index | Measure | Index |
| Economic productivity P$ | 1.40 | 100 | 1.27 | 90 | 1.00 | 71 | 0.83 | 59 |
| Economic productivity of labor, P$(L | 4.53 | 100 | 3.98 | 88 | 3.11 | 69 | 2.85 | 63 |
| Economic productivity of capital, P$(K) | 2.63 | 100 | 2.38 | 91 | 1.85 | 70 | 1.47 | 56 |
| Economic productivity of programmed fixed cost P$(PFC) | 8.89 | 100 | 8.36 | 94 | 7.04 | 79 | 6.31 | 71 |

Figure 16 summarizes economic productivity data over the previous five years. This data had never before been seen. Value added had never been calculated. Costs had never been assembled in this way. With this data company decision makers saw where the profit problem was coming from. For five years, variable costs had been rising faster than sales revenue. So value added was increasing slower than sales revenue. For five years, people costs, capital costs, and programmed fixed costs—the company's fixed costs—had been rising much faster than the value added dollars needed to pay these costs.

In year 5 fixed costs were slightly more than value added, resulting in an economic loss of $381 thousand. The company, however, reported a profit for the year. The profit resulted from lower capital costs calculated by accounting rules. For economic productivity the company calculated capital costs using the method shown in Figure 2. This method results in capital costs higher than when calculated by accounting rules.

The proposed budget for year 6 projected a significant loss. What should the company do? One thing they did was to prepare this economic productivity study. The study was easy to do. A cost accountant or a financial analyst can prepare the data in a morning's work, or less. And with this data the company had information they had never seen before. They had never seen:

- Total people costs and the trend of these costs
- Total capital costs and the trend of these costs
- Total programmed fixed costs and the trend of these costs
- Total fixed costs (the total of people costs, capital costs, and programmed fixed costs), and the trend of these costs
- Total variable costs and the trend of these costs
- Value added, and the trend of value added

They did, of course, have data on total sales revenue but had not been monitoring the trend of total sales revenue. Managers, however, did know something of the trend from seeing data on sales revenue each reporting period. Now they had data on all these economic measures for the past five years. And with the proposed budget they had a projection for the budget year ahead. If they had been tracking these numbers monthly, they would have seen a profit problem developing during year two. Acting then, the problem would have been easier to fix.

Company A had never calculated value added. But the company has to earn these value added dollars to pay its fixed costs. Value added dollars more than fixed costs is operating income. Value added dollars less than fixed costs is operating loss.

Value added begins with the value added in each sale, each transaction. Each sale, each transaction has its variable costs. Each also has a selling price. The difference between the selling price and the variable costs for what was sold is the value added. Total value added can be increased by:

1. Increasing sales revenue

2. Increasing average value added percent, using the audit method illustrated in Figure 4

3. Reducing some variable costs, by:

- Reductions in purchase prices of one or more of the materials, parts, components, and energy used in producing the products sold
- Redesign selected products using the principles of value engineering
- Substituting alternate, higher value added products

4. Increasing some prices

5. Selling more of the products with higher value added.

Having the data shown in the Figure 4, the product line audit spreadsheet, company people will find ways to improve the company's average value added percent.

Looking at the data shown in Figure 15 we see the key measures of economic productivity and how they have changed over the last five years. Purchases of materials, parts, and components used in producing the products sold have increased faster than sales revenue. So value added has grown more slowly than sales revenue. Total fixed costs (L + K + PFC) have grown much more rapidly than value added. So operating income has dropped sharply, falling slightly negative in year 5. The year 5 close, however, did show a slight profit since the accounting costs of capital are lower than the Company P&L Economics costs of capital.

In Figure 15 we calculate economic productivity by dividing value added by the total of L + K + PFC. For year 1, for example, we calculate economic productivity by dividing value added ($84,853) by the total of L + K + PFC ($60,507) to get an economic productivity figure of 140. This figure is not useful on its own, but is very informative in how it changes over time.

Whether by the accounting record, or the Company P&L Economics record, operating income was much less than satisfactory. What to do?

In Figure 16, we see economic productivity falling from 100 in year 1 to 90 in year 3 and to 71 in year 5. At the time this study was made, the company was preparing its budget for year 6, with the budget figures indicating a further decline to 59 in year 6. The partial measures show similar declines:

|  | Year 1 | Year 3 | Year 5 | Year 6 |
|---|---|---|---|---|
| Economic Productivity P$ | 100 | 90 | 71 | 59 |
| Economic Productivity Of Labor P$(L) | 100 | 88 | 69 | 63 |
| Economic Productivity Of Capital P$(K) | 100 | 91 | 70 | 56 |
| Economic Productivity of Programmed Fixed Costs P$(PFC) | 100 | 94 | 79 | 71 |

## ACTIONS TAKEN

None of the information shown in Figures 14, 15, and 16 was known by Company A's management and decision-makers until this study was made. All the needed data was in the division's chart of accounts. But the data was never assembled this way until the division's people learned about Company P&L Economics. Now they had new information on what had been developing over the past six years. They also had information on corrective actions needed.

If Company A had been using Company P&L Economics over this entire six years, they would have seen the operating income problem developing in year 2, and could have begun corrective actions then, when fixes would have been much easier, and quicker.

Actions taken included:

1. Analysis of value added by product, using the procedure described in Figure 4, Product Line Audit Spreadsheet. Using this spreadsheet data, division people found ways to improve average value added, by:

   1. Reducing the variable costs for some products
   2. Redesigning some products using the principles of value engineering
   3. In some cases, substituting a high value added product for a low value added product
   4. Increasing sales efforts on high value added products
   5. Raising some product prices
   6. Fixing high volume, low value added products by some combination of the actions listed above

   Within a few months average value added percent began to improve.

2. Sales people found significant opportunities to increase sales of some of the high value added products.

3. For new products, sales and product development people set goals for sales revenue. They also set goals for value added percents significantly higher than the current average.

4. Sales people identified major customers and major prospects in their sales territories. These were the 20% of all customers and prospects who typically account for about 80% of all sales revenue. For these major customers and prospects, sales people developed sales plans and actions to be taken by themselves and

other company people, as appropriate. The company organized additional professional sales training for their sales people. This training included the principles and methods described in this book in the section on creating and keeping customers. Improved sales and marketing was an important part of the company's profit improvement process.

5.  In addition to their goals for sales revenue, sales people set goals also for value added. Marketing and sales people became business people as well as sales people. They set goals for sales revenue. They also set goals for the value added in that sales revenue.

6.  Goals for value added dollars, and goals for average value added percent became a part of the company's incentive compensation plan.

7.  Manufacturing worked on productivity improvement using the methods of lean manufacturing to increase productivity, improve quality, and increase output to support increased sales without requiring significant new investment.

This combination of actions worked successfully. In nine months average value added percent increased seven percentage points, sales revenue increased more than ten percent, and operating income was satisfactory.

## IMPORTANT IDEAS IN CHAPTER 9
## ECONOMIC PRODUCTIVITY

1.  The first line in the income statement, Sales Revenue, is the first measure of company, or business unit, success. In successful companies, managing the top line is an important part of managing the bottom line.

2.  The measure of economic productivity (P$) is useful for planning present actions to achieve desired operating income. The formula for Economic Productivity:

$$P\$ = \frac{VA}{L + K + PFC}$$

3. Value added is total sales revenue minus the variable costs incurred to produce the products sold. Value added is the value created by the company.

4. The company is a structure of people, capital, and programmed fixed costs. The job of this structure is to produce value added. Value added dollars pay for the cost of this structure (total fixed costs). After total fixed costs are paid, the balance is operating income.

5. There may be hundreds or thousands of line item fixed cost accounts. Managers manage all of these accounts, one at a time. Managing all of them one at a time does not manage the total of all of them. Today's management of fixed costs leaves total fixed costs unmanaged, and uncontrolled.

6. Unless they are using Company P&L Economics, managers do not see:

- Total people costs and the trend of these costs
- Total capital costs and the trend of these costs
- Total programmed fixed costs and the trend of these costs
- Total fixed costs (people costs + capital costs + programmed fixed costs) and the trend of total fixed costs
- Value added, and the trend of value added. Value added pays fixed costs, and after fixed costs are paid, the balance is operating income
- Operating income including higher capital costs, and the trend of this operating income

# Chapter 10

# Key Performance Areas that Determine
# Every Company's Success

Peter Drucker, in his 1954 mind-expanding book, *The Practice of Management,* emphasized that management must be focused on much more than the bottom line. Profitability is essential. But profitability is only one of the key performance areas that determine every company's success. Emphasis on profitability, without emphasizing also these other key areas, will not lead the company to its desired success. Drucker wrote:

"To emphasize only profit misdirects managers to the point where they may endanger the survival of the business. To obtain profit today they tend to undermine the future." [1]

He then went on to describe all the key performance areas that determine every company's success:

1. Market standing
2. Innovation
3. Productivity
4. Physical and financial resources
5. Profitability

**6.** Manager performance and development
**7.** Worker performance and attitude
**8.** Public responsibility

Profitability was only one of eight key performance areas defined by Peter Drucker in his 1954 book. The world of business enterprise and its environments have evolved for more than half a century since Drucker defined these key performance areas. Change has happened. We now live and work in a world evolving at a Moore's Law rate of change. Drucker's 1954 list of the key performance areas that determine every company's success is still a good list. But some adjustments make it a more useful list for today's fast changing world:

| Peter Drucker's Key Performance Areas | Key Performance Areas for Today |
|---|---|
| 1. Market position | 1. Creating and keeping customers |
| 2. Productivity | 2. Quality and productivity |
| 3. Innovation | 3. Innovation |
| 4. Physical and financial resource | 4. Physical and financial resources |
| 5. Profitability | 5. Profitability |
| 6. Manager performance and Development | 6. Organization capability |
| 7. Worker performance and attitude | 7. Public responsibility |
| 8. Public responsibility | 8. Environmental responsibility |

## 1. CREATING AND KEEPING CUSTOMERS

The purpose of every company is to create value for its customers. A statement of company purpose will state what values to what customers. The task of marketing and sales, then, is to create and keep those customers. Successful companies will be leaders in how they create and keep customers. They will be more successful than their peers in gaining market position.

In today's globalized world, global market share is a useful measure of success in creating and keeping customers in only a few industries, including automobiles, oil and gas, coal, steel, ship building, power generating equipment, and polymers.

In a globalized world, market share may be difficult to measure for most companies. But all companies can measure their position in relation to their competitors. Company sales people know the competitive situation in their sales areas. Company sales people can reliably evaluate their company's position in relation to the company's competitors using the procedure described in Figure 7.

There are useful measures of the company's success in creating and keeping customers. If market share data are available, as in the auto industry, that is the best method for measuring success in creating and keeping customers. If market share data are not available, useful information can be found in competitive comparisons. Company sales people can evaluate company competitive position in relation to competitors. This relationship can be rated numerically, such as: 2/10, indicating that our company is number 2 of 10 competitors. Figure 4 includes the estimating of this measure.

A company's success in creating and keeping customers increases sales revenue and value added.

## 2. QUALITY AND PRODUCTIVITY

After World War II, W. Edwards Deming taught statistical quality control to the Japanese. The Japanese were quick learners, and developed quality technologies further. Toyota was one of the companies most effectively developing quality technology. The result was that Toyota became a quality leader, and the Toyota production system (TPS), became a model for quality and productivity excellence. TPS spread through the manufacturing world, continuing to evolve and improve.

The TPS ideas that improved quality and productivity in manufacturing also improve quality and productivity in other industries, and in other areas of work. Wherever work is done, and whatever the kind of work, there is opportunity for continuous quality and productivity improvement. The TPS ideas evolved into "lean" manufacturing, and "lean" operations in all other kinds of work.

Lean operations, producing output satisfying customer expectations, without error, without waste, improves both quality and productivity. Today, quality and productivity technologies combine to satisfy customer expectations without error, without waste.

Productivity is the measure of how efficiently the work is done. Productivity measures can be used In every area of company activity. An individual productivity measure has little value, unless it can be compared with some similar measure. Individual productivity measures tell us how the measure changes over time. What matters is the trend of the measure over time, always aiming for continuous improvement. The basic formula is very simple:

$$\text{Productivity} = \frac{\text{Output}}{\text{Inputs}}$$

Output is what the work produces. Inputs are the resources used to produce the output. To calculate total productivity, the formula looks like this:

$$P = \frac{O}{L + K + M + E}$$

P = Total productivity
O = Output from the work done
L = Total people inputs
K = Total capital inputs
M = Total materials inputs (materials, parts, and all other components used in producing the output)
E = Total energy inputs
Output and inputs can be expressed in units or in dollars.

Units are always preferable, whenever output and all the factors can be measured in units. When they can't be measured in units, dollars can be used. More widely used are the partial measures: productivity of labor, productivity of capital, productivity of materials, and productivity of energy:

$$P = \frac{O}{L} \qquad P = \frac{O}{K} \qquad P = \frac{O}{M} \qquad P = \frac{O}{E}$$

## 3. INNOVATION

Creating and keeping customers and quality and productivity create business success today. Innovation creates future business success. Innovation builds the future of the company. One of the basic principles in quality for all areas of work is the simple statement: there is always a better way. Innovation discovers and develops and successfully markets these better ways.

Google gave us a better way to find information.

Apple gave us a better way to compute and communicate with their iPad and their iPhone

Face Book gave us a better way of communicating with friends

Automobile companies are beginning to give us better ways to eliminate harmful emissions

Start-ups are introducing non-polluting energy sources

Companies continuously improve their products and services, continually developing better ways

Non-polluting energy sources are an innovation response to the need to restore and maintain a human-healthy biosphere. More and more we will need innovative ways to:

(1) Deal with change happening in the biosphere

(2) Help restore and maintain a human-healthy biosphere

Innovation will create our future.

## 4. PHYSICAL AND FINANCIAL RESOURCES

The company's physical and financial resources are the capital investments incurred by management decision to establish and operate the enterprise. These include land, buildings, capital equipment, software, and all the digital technologies that have changed and expanded the company's capabilities.

The company's physical and financial resources combine with, and enable, the

company's human resources to accomplish the purpose of the enterprise. Company people using the company's capital resources create the organization, and the company, capability. Goals and performance measures for physical and financial resources are needed to accomplish company goals.

## 5. PROFITABILITY

Profitability is essential for maintaining and continuously improving present operations, and for creating the desired future for the company. Company P&L Economics, the economics of the business enterprise, is a technology very useful for managing company revenue, costs, and profitability. This book explains the concepts, the methods, and the measures of this new economics, with application examples.

## 6. ORGANIZATION CAPABILITY

Organization capability enables the company to do what it was organized to do. The company's people use the company's physical and financial resources to create value for customers. That is what the company is organized to do—create value for customers. Organization capability, using the company's physical and financial resources, creates that value for customers. Value added is the measure of the value created for customers. Increasing organization capability increases the company's ability to create value added.

What the company earns from what it does is the value added in sales revenue. Company P&L Economics increases the capability of the organization to manage sales revenue, variable costs, value added, and fixed costs to achieve desired operating income. Operating income is the source of company profit.

## 7. PUBLIC RESPONSIBILITY

The company exists and operates in a social environment, now global. This global social environment has grown and evolved from a long history of individual countries and cultures. With globalization, all countries and cultures inter-relate. Economies inter-relate. Economically, everything relates to everything else.

Bank failures in small countries can affect big countries. Economics is global. Social problems and population problems in one country or area affect others. "The public" changes and evolves, fast. What is the company's public responsibility? First of all, the company's responsibility is jobs. Good jobs. And in addition to good jobs, public responsibility requires good citizenship behavior.

Company P&L Economics gives decision-makers a much better understanding of revenue, costs, value added, and operating income. With this knowledge, decision makers develop profitable operations, maintain good jobs, and have the resources for supporting civic needs.

## 8. ENVIRONMENTAL RESPONSIBILITY

We were 2.5 billion people living on planet Earth in 1950. We are now (2012) 7 billion. There are consequences from all these people, their industry, their agriculture, and their real estate development, existing and working on planet Earth. The consequences are degrading the biosphere which is our home. And this 7 billion will increase to 9 billion by mid-century, and to 10 billion by 2100. Nature responds to the changes happening in the biosphere with global warming ($CO_2$ in the atmosphere now 395ppm--up more than a third--and rising at a rate of about 2 ppm/year), causing changing climates, rising sea levels, and a sixth great extinction of secies. What people cause, people can cure. But will we? Actions needed include:

1. Conserve the biosphere!
2. Limit "development" to areas already developed
3. Remediate damage already done to the biosphere

4. Stop harmful emissions and waste into the biosphere—the Earth's atmosphere, land, and water.

5. Extract and reuse, or neutralize, or destroy, harmful emissions and wastes already in the biosphere.

Whatever we do, nature responds by its own laws, which have no concern for human costs, or human laws, or human needs and wants. Science has learned much about nature's laws. One thing we learn is that nature's laws prevail.

We can't stop nature from doing what nature does. But we can stop ourselves from doing what we do that causes nature to increasingly warm planet Earth, increasingly threatening our existence on planet Earth. We are beginning to talk about slowing down what we do that causes nature to act as nature is acting. And it costs too much. Nature's response continues.

The task ahead: Work out how to support huge and growing human populations and conserve the biosphere. Aim to reverse population growth and move toward a sustainable human population on planet Earth.

## COMPANY PURPOSE: THE GUIDE FOR EVERYTHING THE COMPANY DOES

Company purpose is the broadly accepted view of what the company is and what it will become, usually expressed in a Statement of Company Purpose. Company purpose states what the company is and does and will become over the next several years. A good statement of purpose drives company performance for a decade or more.

1. The Ford motor car company began operations in 1906, its purpose, to build a car that anyone could buy. Henry Ford invented the assembly line and built a low-cost car that put America on wheels and made Ford the leading car company for two decades.

2. McCaw Cellular, 1984, its purpose, to build a phone company that connects people to people instead of people to places. In a world of land lines connecting people to places, Craig McCaw

saw opportunity in connecting people to people. In the early 1980s, he participated in the FCC lottery for cellular licenses and bought the rights of other winners. Using his cable company to finance expansion, he built a nation-wide cellular service before the established land line companies noticed what was happening. In 1994, McCaw sold McCaw Cellular to AT&T for $11.5 billion.

3. Google, 1998, its purpose, to organize the world's information and make it universally accessible and useful. Started in a garage, with one employee, twelve years later Google was a $22 billion business. Purpose that is right for the company and right for the times, can bring great success.

Companies think of their purpose in many ways:
The purpose of our company is to make money
The purpose of our company is to create wealth for its stockholders
The purpose of our company is to be number one in our markets
The purpose of our company is to be a leader in our industry
The purpose of our company is to be the best producer of cement (or whatever it is that the company produces)
The purpose of our company is to grow 10% a year

Statements of purpose asserting that the company will be the best in its products or its profitability do not help the company be the best. Company people do not relate their work to such statements of purpose.

## FINDING PURPOSE IS A TWO-PART JOB

Without an effective statement of purpose, or with an ineffective statement of purpose, company people have no guide for their thinking and actions. A good statement of purpose helps get all company people working together for company success now, next month, next year, next many years. This chapter proposes a kind of purpose that can drive company success over a span of years. Finding purpose is a two-part job:

Part 1. Developing a short statement of purpose, stating what it is that can build company success for a decade or more. A statement of the company purpose can be useful, but it is not enough. Also needed is a Part 2.

Part 2. The near-term goals and performance measures in some combination of the key performance areas that will move the company toward its purpose. Peter Drucker defined eight areas as the areas that determine every company's success. Modifying his list slightly to make it more timely for today gives us the following listing. These are key areas determining company success:

1. Creating and Keeping Customers
2. Quality and Productivity
3. Innovation
4. Profitability
5. Organization Capability
6. Physical and Financial Resources
7. Public Responsibility
8. Environmental Responsibility

Leaders of existing companies can stand in the shoes of entrepreneurs and think creatively about the purpose of their company. It would be wise, too, to involve other company people in this creative thinking. With knowledge of company operations up to now, and with knowledge of the world outside where company success is created, an inspiring purpose can be found. However, change happens continuously in the world we live in and work in. A long-lived company will at times, transition into a changed purpose:

In the 1800s, Studebaker made wagons renowned for their reliability and ruggedness. After the Civil War, Studebaker's rugged Conestoga wagons carried settlers west, across the country. As cars and trucks replaced wagons, demand for wagons withered. In 1902, Studebaker repurposed to become a manufacturer of cars that were uniquely rugged and durable. The Studebaker "Big 6" was a leading touring car in the 1920s. After World War II, Studebaker missed a needed repurposing, and died.

Ford, 1906, purpose: Build a car that everyone can buy. Henry Ford invented the assembly line, built and sold the Model T at one-third the cost of other cars, put America on wheels, and made Ford the leading car company for two decades. What is Ford's purpose today?

NASA, 1961, purpose: Land a man on the moon by the end of the decade, and return him safely to the Earth. On July 26, 1969, Neil Armstrong and Buzz Aldrin stepped off the lunar module, Eagle, onto the surface of the moon. After 21 hours on the moon, they piloted Eagle back to the command module, Columbia, orbiting the moon, and returned safely to Earth. NASA's current purpose lacks the power of direction. Its purpose, "to pioneer the future in space exploration, scientific discovery, and aeronautics research."

Web start-ups always start with a purpose. Those few whose purpose satisfies enough users become quick successes:

Google, 1998, its purpose, to organize the world's information and make it universally accessible and useful.

Facebook, 2003, its purpose, to help Harvard students communicate with each other.

A good statement of purpose is right for the company and right for the times. It applies the present and planned capabilities of the company to a stated competitive advantage that can build the company over a period of years. The statement is clear and easy to understand. It creates interest and excitement and inspires and coordinates high performance toward the achievement of the stated purpose.

Once found, company purpose becomes a symbol for the company. It appears on company documents. A plan and a budget begins with the company purpose. Proposals of all kinds begin with a statement of the company purpose. For an investment proposal, traditionally an ROI figure has been the most important consideration. Now, the company purpose is the first and most important consideration. For any new investment, the first question is not, "What is the ROI?" The first question is "How important is this new investment to the achievement of company purpose?"

The president of a manufacturing corporation at budget time received Division requests for new investments totaling over $300 million. All showed discounted rates of return higher than the company's threshold minimum. Which should be accepted? The company expected to be able to finance about $180 million. This company did have a written statement of purpose. A director suggested that the president prioritize the proposals according to how important they were for achieving the company's purpose. This evaluation quickly identified the $180 million most important.

Everything the company does, its plans, its budgets, its investments, its actions, contributes to the achievement of company purpose. Company purpose is always on the table when decisions are made; always in the minds of company people in the work they do. It's everywhere in view; on bulletin boards, computer screens, in advertising and promotion, on documents, web sites, signs, reports; everywhere.

What matters is achieving the company purpose. And what matters now, is the goals and measures in Part 2 of company purpose, the near-term goals and performance measures that will move the company toward its Purpose.

Watching the Environment

While striving for company purpose, companies will perceptively search the company's environments for any changes that will help or hurt their progress. The company's purpose and its profitability are created in the world outside the company, in the commercial, technical, economic, political, social, educational, and internet environments, and the ecological environment. All of these environments are changing, rapidly. Companies will be alert to developing changes in the environments they work in to identify:

(1) Changes that can help them achieve their purpose.

(2) Changes that can limit the achievement of their purpose, and take appropriate actions.

(3) Changes that require a reevaluation and redirection of company purpose.

Purpose and Company P&L Economics

Purpose directs the company in everything the company does. The company produces products, delivers services. The company creates and keeps customers. The company innovates. The company continuously improves. The company develops its people. The company employs the people and the capital needed to accomplish its purpose. And in doing all of this the company needs to earn a profit, for:

- Maintaining and improving present operations
- Creating the company's future
- Rewarding investors
- Appropriate incentive compensation, broadly awarded

Company P&L Economics helps managers and all decision makers manage revenue and costs to create the desired operating income.

## IMPORTANT IDEAS IN CHAPTER 10
## KEY PERFORMANCE AREAS THAT DETERMINE EVERY COMPANY'S SUCCESS

1. More than half a century ago Peter Drucker defined eight key performance areas that determine every company's success. Drucker's list is still a good list. But after more than fifty years of Moore's Law rate of change in companies and their environments, the following modified listing is better for our times:

   1. Creating and Keeping Customers
   2. Quality and Productivity
   3. Innovation
   4. Physical and Financial Resources
   5. Profitability
   6. Organization Capability
   7. Public Responsibility
   8. Environmental Responsibility

2. Creating and keeping customers, and quality and productivity, create business success today.

3. Innovation creates future business success. Innovation builds the future of the company. Innovation will create our future.

4. More and more we will need innovative ways to:

   (1) Deal with change happening in the biosphere
   (2) Help restore and maintain a human-healthy biosphere

5. Organization capability enables the company to do what it was organized to do. The company's people use the company's physical and financial resources to create value for customers. That is what the company is organized to do—create value for customers. Value added is the measure of value created for customers.

6. The world is now home to 7 billion people. There are consequences from all these people, their industry, their agriculture, and their real estate development; all living and working on planet Earth. Those consequences are now degrading the biosphere that is our home. Nature responds, with global warming, changing climates, rising sea levels, a sixth great extinction. What people cause, people can cure. But will we? Actions needed include:

   1. Conserve the biosphere!
   2. Limit "development" to areas already developed
   3. Remediate damage already done to the biosphere
   4. Stop harmful emissions and wastes into the biosphere—the Earth's atmosphere, land, and water.
   5. Extract and reuse, or neutralize, or destroy, harmful emissions and wastes already in the biosphere.

7. We can't stop nature from doing what nature does. But we can stop ourselves from doing what we do that causes nature to act in ways threatening our existence on planet Earth.

8. Articulate a Company Purpose that guides everything the company does. Finding company purpose is a two-part job:

   Part 1. Developing a short statement of purpose, stating what it is that can build company success for a decade or more
   Part 2. Setting near-term goals and performance measures in some combination of the key performance areas that will move the company toward its purpose

References:
[1] Drucker, Peter F., *The Practice of Management*, Harper & Row, New York, NY, 1954
[2] Zay Jeffries, General Electric scientist, undated notes on personal conversation, about 1957
[3] Joel Dean, *Managerial Economics*, Prentice-Hall, Inc., Englewood Cliffs, NJ, 1951
[4] William Christopher, *Better Budgeting, How Continuous Plans and Budgets Create Enduring Success*